'I encourage everyone to take an interest in nurturing our native gardens and parklands in this beautiful country of ours. This book is a must-have for anyone who is keen to preserve our native environment.'

—JAMIE DURIE

Other books by Robin Stewart

Non-fiction titles for adults

Being Mike Abbott
The Clean House Effect
Envirocat
Chemical-Free Home
Chemical-Free Pest Control
Chasing Rainbows
The Dog Book
Australian Green Home and Garden
Tread Lightly: A Guide to Travelling Green in Australia

Children's books

Moonbird
New Faces: The Complete Book of Alternative Pets (Children's Book Council of Australia – Information Book of the Year 1995)
Wombat: Bush Babies Solo Series
Koala: Bush Babies Solo Series
Charles Darwin's Big Idea (shortlisted for the Children's Book Council of Australia Eve Pownall Award 2006)
Darwin's Tortoise
A Life in the Wild (Volumes 1 & 2)

from SEEDS *to* LEAVES

from SEEDS *to* LEAVES

Doug & Robin Stewart

Published by Black Inc.,
an imprint of Schwartz Books Pty Ltd
Wurundjeri Country
22-24 Northumberland Street
Collingwood VIC 3066, Australia
enquiries@blackincbooks.com
www.blackincbooks.com

First published by Agmedia in 1995
This edition published in 2021; reprinted in 2025

9781760643218 (paperback)
9781921866333 (ebook)

A catalogue record for this
book is available from the
National Library of Australia

Cover design by Thomas Deverall
Cover images: photolibrary
Illustrations on pages 25, 50, 83, 93, 102, 117, 131, 145 by Jenny Bullock
All other illustrations by Doug Stewart

Printed in Australia by McPherson's Printing Group.

Contents

Seeds

The seeds I sowed –
For weeks unseen –
Have pushed up pygmy
Shoots of green;
So frail you'd think
The tiniest stone
Would never let
A glimpse be shown.

But no; a pebble
Near them lies,
At least a cherry-stone
In size,
Which that mere sprout
Has heaved away,
To bask in sun,
And see the day.

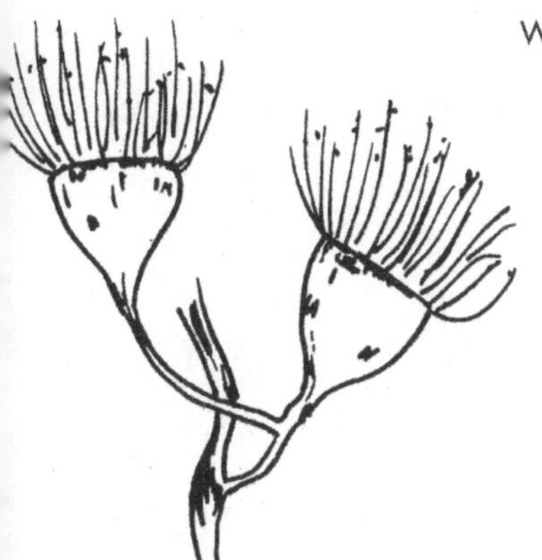

Walter de la Mare

Preface

Seed is the germ of life, a genetic blueprint that has the potential to grow into an astonishing variety of plant life.

When it comes to seed, Nature is generous – so generous that we are given opportunity upon opportunity to mend the damaging effects of unwise agricultural, mining and land management practice.

Australia is an ancient land mass that has been isolated from other continents for tens of millions of years. Our continent is composed of fragile, highly leached soils bound together by unique, varied and extraordinarily beautiful flora, including botanical curiosities of international fame, such as kangaroo paw, Sturt desert pea, banksias, waratahs, dryandras and black boys.

The conservation of our natural heritage requires careful management of our national parks, State forests and reserves, as well as the involvement of every Australian. We need long-term plans to solve critical environmental problems brought about by a mere two hundred years of white settlement.

Take a moment to imagine the concept of every Australian viewing every seed of every native plant as something precious, a life-form to be nurtured. Visualise a network of trees and shrubs linking city and country people, a green web weaving its way across our continent: wildlife corridors to preserve the wealth of our fauna and flora.

To take part in this miracle of regeneration, a simple container is all you need, for Nature provides the seed, soil, air, moisture and warmth required for germination. It will be your privilege to witness the growth of a plant from seedling stage through to flowering and seeding.

It doesn't matter if your contribution is large or small, for every seed counts. You may choose to grow native plants for your suburban garden, or you may decide to participate in a community-based conservation project.

Every single plant is important in the overall greening of our nation; every native seed represents a challenge. Will you help nurture our natural heritage?

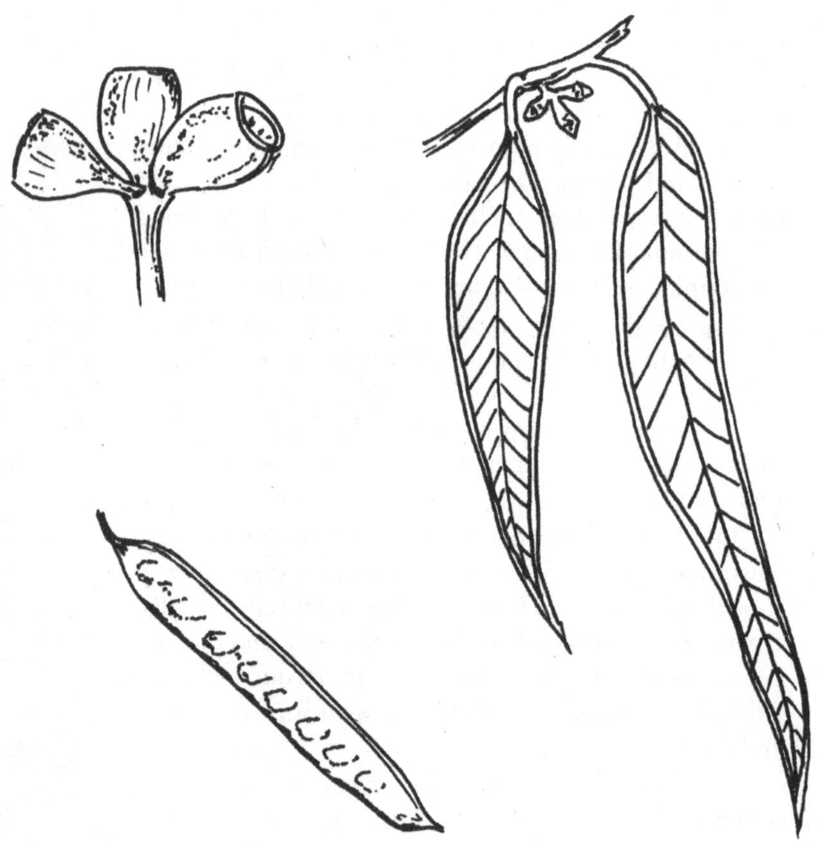

Introduction: The challenge of climate change

Nature on the move: the new reality

Climate change is now an accepted reality that requires all of us to alter our ways and consider the environment a top priority. The wider aspects of global warming (such as melting icecaps, rising sea-levels and climate-change politics) are well covered in other books. Our primary focus will therefore be on native vegetation and the manner in which climate change affects the grasses, shrubs and trees that make up our unique ecosystems.

Everyone is familiar with the migration habits of birds and butterflies, but most people are unaware that plant species migrate too, sometimes over great distances, in order to survive.

The creation of migration corridors is vital for the survival of many plant species. Seeds need pathways along which to disperse. Pathways free of invasive weeds; pathways that offer a network of escape routes along, for example, creeks, rivers and roadsides; and pathways big enough to allow the random seeding so typical of many plants. Animal, bird, reptile, frog and insect refugees will also travel these climate-change highways, escaping from environments that were previously suitable, but which are now perhaps too warm and dry.

A race against time

Global warming requires that evolution speed up, well beyond its normal gradual rate. Climate change is warming up our planet and in doing so is forcing vegetation to move from familiar habitats to places where it has never grown before.

Some species will not be able to adapt to such rapid change and will become extinct. This is already happening. Some plants and animals will have no opportunity to migrate. In alpine ecosystems, for instance, plants will find it impossible to move higher up the mountain if they are already growing at the top! Plants indigenous to remote islands may be unable to escape due to the barrier of surrounding oceans. Other species will have their escape routes blocked off by mountain ranges, large lakes, deserts, farm-land or polluted cities.

But there will be winners, too. Some grasses, shrubs and trees will be able to expand their range, especially in northern Australia where rainfall is increasing. Some plants will migrate successfully, and some will be helped by human endeavours such as artificial seeding and mass plantings. But it will be a race against time. New ecosystems will evolve; other, more fragile ecosystems will collapse.

Our role: anyone can plant a tree

Because global warming is the result of human influence, it seems only fair that people work hard to give every species

(plant and animal) the best possible chance of survival. If we don't, invasive weeds and feral animals will run rampant, erosion and salinity will be growing problems, skeletal trees will be commonplace, many species will become extinct, and we'll lose – forever – valuable plant and animal biodiversity.

Talk of global warming, climate change and the clearing of old-growth forests can leave us feeling depressed and helpless. However, anyone can plant a tree. A long-lived tree will soak up carbon dioxide, which will help reduce global warming, one hopes for decades to come. This simple act offers hope for the future. It's an opportunity for positive change: admittedly minute, yet at the same time significant.

Planting a native garden is becoming more and more relevant. You may have noticed that the length of the growing season, flowering and nesting times, and the migratory patterns of local birds are changing in response to climate change. You may also have noticed that some plants have either died or are struggling to keep pace with the changing climate. Perhaps they can't cope with the prolonged dry, have been uprooted or had branches ripped off by fierce storms, or simply don't thrive any more due to milder winters and earlier springs. Increased pollution and more vigorous insect and fungal attacks could also be having an adverse effect.

Now is a good time to replace these struggling species with plants able to thrive in a changed environment: deep-rooted native trees and shrubs, preferably with strong limbs and leaf canopies with natural resistance to insect and fungal attack. These trees will be better able to withstand drought, heavy rain and windstorms.

Take a walk around your area. Which native trees and shrubs (not necessarily indigenous to the area) have survived the changed conditions without watering or pampering? Do they have viable seed? If so, collect this seed and begin a special 'bank' of survivor-type seed for future planting. Sometimes these survivor plants will come from an adjoining climatic region. The collection of seeds from native trees growing in an adjacent warmer, drier area may also be a good idea.

Perhaps your garden will become part of a wildlife corridor. If so, choose your native plants with this in mind, create frog ponds, provide birdbaths and position hollow logs for lizards.

Climate-change highways: linking rainforests and deserts

Already, many communities are discovering the power of seeds to rejuvenate our environment. In Victoria's Wimmera region, a vegetation corridor (named Project Hindmarsh) has been created, linking the Big and Little Desert National Parks of north-west Victoria. Over 3000 volunteers, including Landcare and community groups, individuals and families, have tackled the enormous task of weed eradication and have planted more than 1.5 million trees, shrubs and native grasses to create a continuous corridor of native bushland. This impressive 2000-kilometre corridor of roadside vegetation – covering a wide climatic region – is allowing vulnerable species such as mallee fowl to migrate south in response to climate change.

Inspired by the success of Project Hindmarsh, Western Australia is in the process of reclaiming land and creating a vegetation link (called the Gondwana Link) between the coast and inland Kalgoorlie. In northern Queensland, meanwhile, the Mount Zero-Taravale Reserve (60 kilometres north-west of Townsville) links drier inland ecosystems to the rainforests of the tropics. The reserve has been designed with climate change in mind. In the event of hotter summers, less reliable rainfall and more severe droughts, these vegetation links will create pathways along which native plants and animals can migrate to more suitable habitats. Within the reserve, over thirty species are considered vulnerable to climate change, including masked

owls, northern bettongs, quolls and southern cassowaries. Spanning steep, rugged mountains, tropical rainforests and flatter, arid country, the reserve protects a remarkable diversity of plant and animal life.

Seed banks: saving our ecological inheritance

Seeds preserve our ecological heritage. On Phillip Island, in southern Victoria, a seed bank (named the Barb Martin Bush-bank) has been established to collect and propagate seed from indigenous vegetation. These have been used to revegetate little penguin and muttonbird rookeries, as well as to create corridors of native vegetation across and around the island, linking patches of remnant vegetation and connecting them to existing networks.

Eucalypts: hardy survivors?

Sometimes seeds throw up surprises. In Mitchell, in inland central Queensland, some indigenous tree species are dying. The cadaghi (*Corymbia torelliana*, previously known as *Eucalyptus torelliana*) shines out as the species most in tune with the changing climate of this arid area. Although a native of the wet tropics of northern Queensland, this tree is grown widely in southern and western Queensland and has survived the drought. More than that, it has thrived without surface watering or special care, to produce a pleasant shade tree that blossoms profusely in November. Honeyeaters, butterflies and bees feast in its blossoms. Its only disadvantage is its tendency to lose limbs. The cadaghi is an example of a successful migrant.

In his book *The Weather Makers*, Tim Flannery predicts that about half of Australia's *Eucalyptus* species will need to migrate in order to survive climate change. Most Australians think of eucalypts as hardy survivors. The majority of species, however, grow in limited geographical areas, within amazingly narrow climate and temperature ranges. Natural and human barriers will make migration either difficult or impossible for many of these species. They will need our help, especially in southern and eastern Australia and Tasmania, where prolonged drought is becoming more and more familiar.

Facing the challenge of climate change

Evolution drives Nature as fast as it can towards adaptation and change. Unfortunately, climate change is galloping ahead at a more rapid rate.

An opportunity exists for us all – as individuals or collectively – to collect native seed and then propagate and plant sufficient trees and shrubs to make a real difference. This book offers easy-to-follow steps to guide you in the process of transforming seeds to leaves.

Can we create a spider's web of climate-change highways throughout Australia – a network of vegetation corridors that will allow native plants and animals to migrate, adapt and survive in our rapidly changing world?

Can *we* act fast enough to manage the climate-change catastrophe that we've created?

Seed collection

Chapter 1

Seed from gardens

Once you begin to collect seed you will look at every Australian tree and shrub in a new light. Your eyes will scan each plant, searching for seed cases – and your mind will be propagating the seed and choosing a place in your garden for the beauty you see before you.

Banksias and dryandras are perhaps the most striking of our native plants, along with the Sturt desert pea. These can be grown from seed and you can collect the cases yourself from the gardens of other enthusiasts.

You will find that you discover botanical treasures in the most amazing places, so always keep secateurs, a few paper bags and a pen in your car.

Seed from bushland

Seed collection is a rewarding pastime, a hobby that is interesting and inexpensive, one that can involve a group of friends or the whole family.

Your time will be spent in pleasant natural surroundings doing something really satisfying – and as a bonus, seed collection should be carried out in fine weather!

In order to find suitable donor trees, plan as follows:

- Establish *why* you are collecting seed. Is it for your garden, a farm shelterbelt, a wildlife corridor, or perhaps for erosion control?
- Is the ground to be planted wet or dry, flat or hilly? What is the soil type?
- Find an area of natural vegetation in a similar locality. Look at the trees and shrubs and decide which you would like to propagate. Remember that local plants will suit local soil and climatic conditions, will require less water and maintenance and will blend with the surroundings and provide invaluable habitat for local wildlife.
- Learn to read seasonal signs, to recognise the cycle of flowering through to the ripeness and availability of seed. You will need to visit the area regularly to check individual species; however, most seed will be collected from early spring through to late summer.
- Identify the species during flowering and mark those trees or shrubs that seem most vigorous and healthy. Heavy flowering usually indicates high yield of seed, and the best specimens nearly always produce the more robust seedlings; so choose your trees carefully.
- Trees in park-like settings usually branch out lower to the ground. These trees will be easier to collect from than forest trees.
- Select an area where there are a number of the same species, and plan to take seed from as many healthy plants as possible.
- Watch your trees carefully as the seed cases mature. Green seed pods or follicles are usually too immature to pick, so wait until they turn brown to black-brown in colour; but hot, dry, windy weather will cause some species (especially the acacias and grevilleas) to drop their seed suddenly, so you will need to watch these plants more closely.

- Acacias, banksias, callistemons, calothamnus, allocasuarinas, casuarinas, eucalypts, hakeas, melaleucas and tea-trees are among the many Australian natives that grow very easily from seed, so set your sights wide!

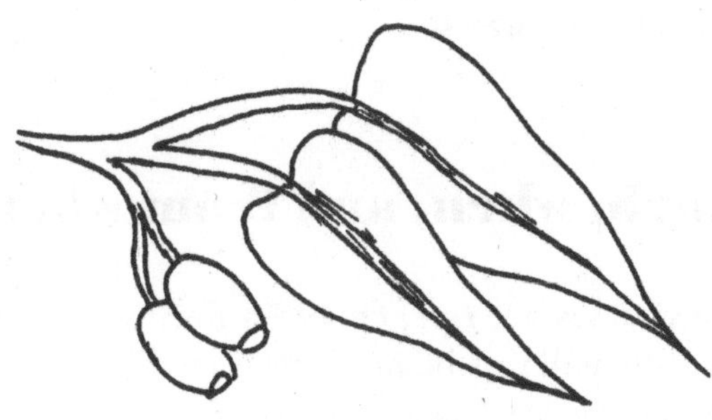

Typical Eucalyptus *with fruit.*

Hickory wattle.

Do you need permission?

Certain species are protected under each State's Flora and Fauna Guarantee Act. Seeds from these species cannot be taken from any public land without a permit; however, they can be collected from private land, with the permission of the owner.

Quarantine restrictions apply to certain plant material being transported between States.

How much, when, and from where?

Once the seed cases are ripe, choose a fine, dry day for your outing. Not only will this be more pleasant for you, but it will also ensure that the seed cases are dry, consequently reducing fungal problems.

Collect from several parts of the same tree, but concentrate on the middle and upper branches if possible, as the seed cases from here will usually be better quality than those lower down. Avoid damage to the tree or shrub.

Do not overcollect: take no more than ten per cent of seed, so that you leave sufficient for the tree itself and for all the insects, birds and animals dependent on the seed supply as food.

Methods and equipment

Seed is normally collected by hand. This can be great fun, especially in the company of good friends. It is best to work in pairs or groups, both for pleasure and safety, especially if you are planning to use ladders or vehicles.

You will need secateurs, labels, and cloth or paper bags. You may also need long-handled tools, for example a long-handled pruning saw.

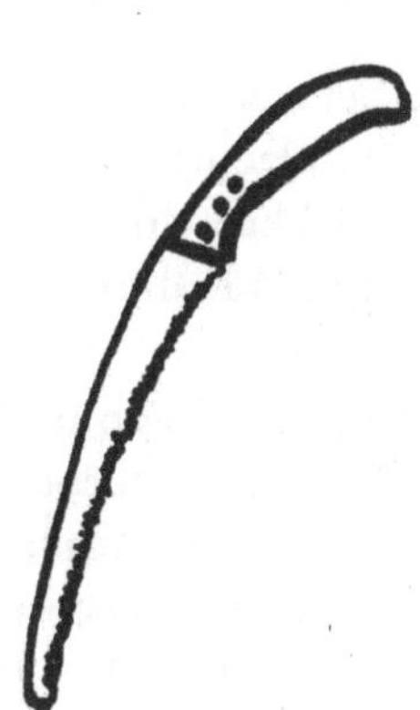

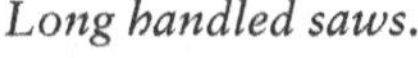

Long handled saws.

Seed from fallen trees and branches

No tree should be cut down specifically for seed; however, if a tree has to be cut down anyway, you may as well harvest the seed. Likewise, if a branch or tree is damaged during a storm, the opportunity should be taken to collect the seed.

Seed that drops naturally

Most pods, berries and fleshy fruit fall when ripe and can be collected by placing beneath the tree, a sheet of plastic or a tarpaulin, weighed down with stones. You may choose to leave the sheeting down for several days, in order to collect the maximum amount.

Either an upside-down umbrella or a large cardboard box makes a good catching receptacle, especially when you give the branches a good shake. Acacias yield well when caught at the optimum time, with pods coming away easily to a light stripping action of the hands. A rake or a stick can be used to lightly beat the higher branches.

Pea-like pods

Acacias, albizias, cassias, hardenbergias, kennedias and other pea-like plants produce pods that split open along two edges when ripe. Hot, windy weather dries and matures the seed, with the pods changing colour from green to brown very rapidly. The pods may even burst open with explosive force.

Your aim should be to collect the seed as the pods begin to dry and split. This will ensure that the seed you collect is mature and long-lasting.

You may also find it worthwhile to pick up seed from the leaf litter beneath the tree, especially if your timing is a bit late. The seed will be hard and shiny black to brown.

Most seed of this type matures from early to late December; however, seasons can vary and so do different localities. A broad range is from mid-spring to late summer.

Fleshy berries

Fleshy berries are found on many plants, including *Acmena* (syn. *Eugenia*) *smithii* (lilly-pilly), *Astroloma humifusum* (cranberry heath) and *Eremophila maculata* (spotted emu bush).

Pittosporums and rainforest fruit

This fleshy fruit falls naturally to the ground, where it is often picked up and eaten by birds or animals. The seed can pass through the animal quite safely, then go on to germinate and grow some distance from the parent plant.

The berries can be gathered from beneath the plant, hand-picked or knocked off with a stick or rake onto a tarpaulin. Each berry will contain one or more seeds embedded in fleshy material, covered and sealed by the skin. Some open to release the seed, but most do not.

Fleshy fruit with a hard stone

Fleshy fruit (similar in type to apricots and peaches) is produced by native plants such as *Macadamia integrifolia*, (smooth-shelled macadamia nut) *Macadamia tetraphylla* (rough-shelled macadamia nut), *Elaeocarpus grandis* (blue quandong), *Santalum lanceolatum* (plum-bush or northern sandalwood), *Ceratopetalum gummiferum* (New South Wales Christmas bush) and *Coprosma hirtella* (currant bush).

These hard-stoned fruits fall to the ground when mature, so they can be gathered from beneath the tree, hand-picked, or knocked down with a stick or rake onto a tarpaulin.

Seed best trapped in a bag

Grevillea, *Boronia*, *Correa* and *Pittosporum* species and *Nuytsia floribunda* (Western Australian Christmas tree) all collect well into a fine pantyhose leg, or a bag of gauze or tough paper (plastic will sweat). Simply place the pantyhose or bag over the ripening fruit and tie firmly around the stem. Remove the bag from the plant when the fruit has matured and shed its seed into the bag. This method ensures that the seed, which tends to be released explosively on ripening, is safely collected.

Grevilleas produce small, light woody pods that ripen rapidly. As the pods burst open, seed is scattered all round the plant. Most ripen from late November to January and expel one or two seeds per pod. Grevillea pods may be picked before they fully mature and will ripen successfully if stored in a paper bag in a warm, dry place.

Boronia seed may also be collected from beneath the plant if the weather is fine and still. Spread sheeting on the ground and hold it in place with stones. The seed will fall naturally when mature.

Seed collected by cutting off mature flower heads

Seed of some native genera can be collected by simply cutting off the fully mature flower head and placing it in a paper bag. These include *Dryandra*, *Isopogon* (cone bush), *Hibiscus*, *Telopea* (waratah), *Patersonia* (native iris), *Anigozanthos* (kangaroo paw) *Blandfordia* (Christmas bells) and many genera of the family *Asteraceae* (daisies).

Daisies need special care to ensure good quality seed free of caterpillar damage and fungal disease. Do not collect during wet weather or after rain, check each flower head for any evidence of caterpillars, and keep the seed quite dry. Cut the flower head from the plant when the centre of the flower becomes loose.

Native iris, kangaroo paw, Christmas bells and hibiscus have capsules that split open when mature. Cut the flower heads carefully and avoid bumping the seed. In nature, seed dispersal is usually triggered by a strong gust of wind.

Each flower head of *Telopea speciosissima* (New South Wales waratah) produces only a few follicles, but each contains many seeds. Collect between the end of March and June in cooler districts, picking those pods that are beginning to turn brown.

Seed collection from hard woody cases

Banksia and hakea seeds are contained in very hard woody follicles, cases that split open on one side only, to release their seed.

Seed of eucalypts, melaleucas, callistemons, calothamnus, angophoras, allocasuarinas, casuarinas, tea-trees and kunzeas is contained in very hard woody capsules, cases that split open along a number of sides to release their seed.

Various methods may be used to harvest these hard woody cases, as follows.

- Use secateurs to snip off twigs holding the cases. Secateurs minimise damage to branches.
- Pick or snip seed cases while standing on the back of a tray truck or utility. Drape the tray with a tarpaulin so that seed cases can simply be dropped and collected later. A rake can also be used to knock down seed cases.
- Climb a ladder and pick the seed cases into a fruit-picking bag, a calico bag or a cardboard box hung around your neck with a strap. This will give you two free hands for picking.
- Climb the tree, using safe climbing shoes, a safety strap and a safety helmet.
- A cherrypicker (a mechanical elevating platform) may be hired by a group. This facilitates safe picking of seed cases alone, without damage to the branches, as it allows pickers to be raised to a convenient level.
- Seed-harvesting machines are used by large companies for the collection of seed from some species.
- In the case of a tree earmarked for felling, you can use a long-handled saw, secateurs or pruner and work from the ground. Cut off the branches bearing the best seed cases, then strip off the cases by hand.
- If a seed-bearing branch high in the tree has suffered storm damage a rope may be used to break the branch right off. Coil a long piece of rope with a heavy stick or stone attached to one end. Throw the rope so that the weighted end goes over the branch. Alternatively, a bow and arrow may be used to shoot heavy-gauge fishing line over the branch, with a rope saw attached. By pulling the rope back and forth you can cut the branch off with the long flexible saw. Use a rubber-tipped arrow to avoid injury.

Work as a team; it will be more fun and much safer. Always keep a first-aid kit handy. Use leather gloves and thick protective clothing when picking seed cases from prickly plants such as some hakeas, *Acacia pulchella* (western prickly Moses) and other plants armed with spines.

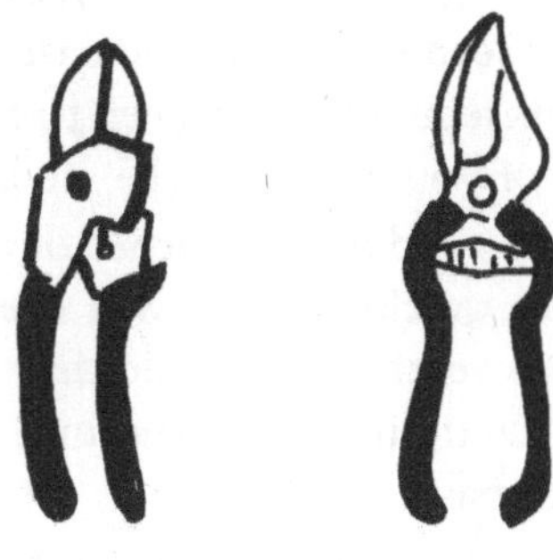

Secateurs.

Selecting the seed cases

The best seed is found in the oldest unopened seed cases, located on the oldest wood.

Aim to cut or break off the mature seed cases only, and avoid cutting or breaking branches that will produce next year's seed crop. After flowering, plants may take several years to fully ripen the seed in their cases. Mature seed is not found in cases that are green: they must be brown or grey in colour.

Most of these cases remain unopened on the plant for an indefinite time. Seed is liberated only after a bushfire, or a prolonged dry season that causes entire branches on the plant to die. On release, the seeds germinate readily after a shower of rain.

Some exceptions to this mode of dispersal and germination include *Banksia coccinea* (scarlet banksia), *Banksia marginata* (silver banksia), *Banksia integrifolia* (coast banksia), *Callistemon viminalis* (weeping bottlebrush), *Callistemon acuminatus* and *Leptospermum laevigatum* (coast tea-tree). These particular plants release their seed while the seed case is still attached to the living plant. Consequently they need to be watched very closely as they ripen, or you may miss the seed.

Seed cases with leaves and twigs attached dry out and release their seed much more quickly. Some will even open within hours of picking if the weather is hot and dry. For this reason small seed cases collected during the summer months should be picked directly into bags.

Banksias produce thick woody cones that need to be removed whole. Ideally, select cones with a few follicles already open. Usually these large, partly embedded woody follicles each contain two thin, winged seeds. Many cones will be without fertilised seed, so select only those containing woody seed cases scattered along the cone.

To test whether the follicle is mature, scrape it with your fingernail. If green or light tan shows through, leave the cone on the plant for a little longer. If dry and woody, it is mature and ready to pick.

Hakeas produce hard, woody fruit that vary from very small to the size of a cricket ball. The dry mature fruit splits open on one side to release two winged seeds, usually dark in colour.

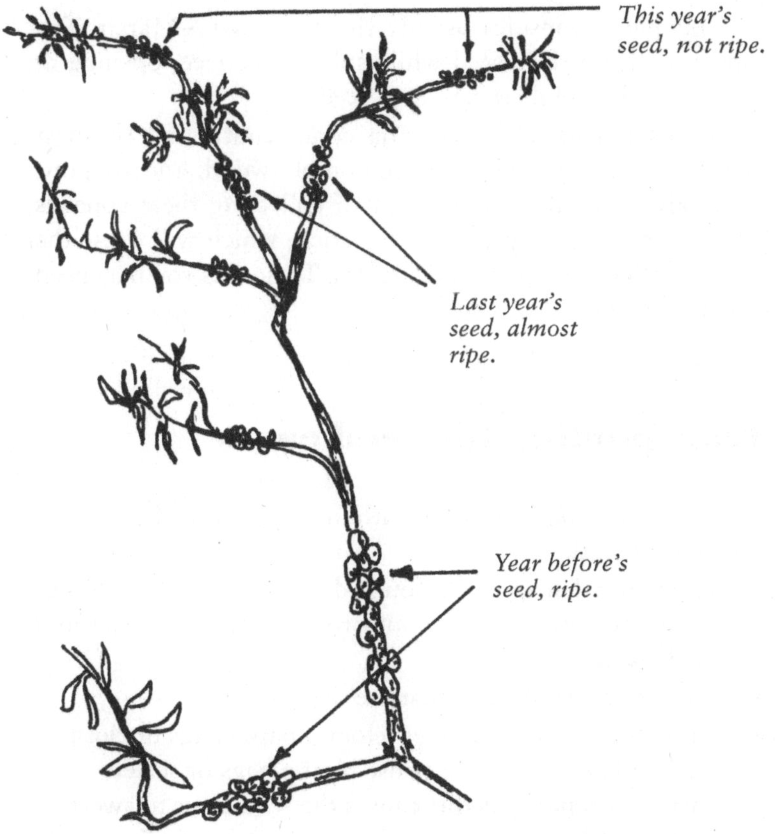

This year's seed, not ripe.

Last year's seed, almost ripe.

Year before's seed, ripe.

Seed capsules: Callistemon.

Seed of eucalypts, melaleucas, callistemons, calothamnus, tea-trees and kunzeas is produced in very large quantities and is very small. Callistemon capsules need to be collected from as far down the plant stem as possible and placed directly into a paper or cloth bag.

Angophora capsules usually ripen February–March. The capsules release their seed while still on the tree, opening at the top to liberate three flat, oval seeds.

Allocasuarina and casuarina cones containing the best quality winged seed will be found on old wood, and are grey, with valves closed. A useful way of collecting these cones is to gently beat the branches with a stick, which will cause the cones to fall onto a waiting tarpaulin. To do this you may need to climb the tree.

Transporting the seed cases

As you collect, *label* every bag with the date, place of collection and type of seed.

Remember that seeds, although dormant, are living things, vulnerable to disease, insect and rodent attack, fungal and mould damage.

- Only collect seed cases that are dry.
- Place seed cases in paper envelopes, paper bags or cloth bags (calico is best). Never use plastic bags or sealed plastic containers, as this causes the seed cases to sweat. Even the driest seed cases will contain a certain degree of moisture, so don't be tempted to use plastic, as mould and fungal attack will certainly destroy the seed.
- Stack your paper and cloth bags into cardboard boxes for the journey home.
- Store the boxes in a dry place until you are ready to extract the seed.

*Jarrah (*E. marginata*).*

*Sugar gum (*E. cladocalyx*).*

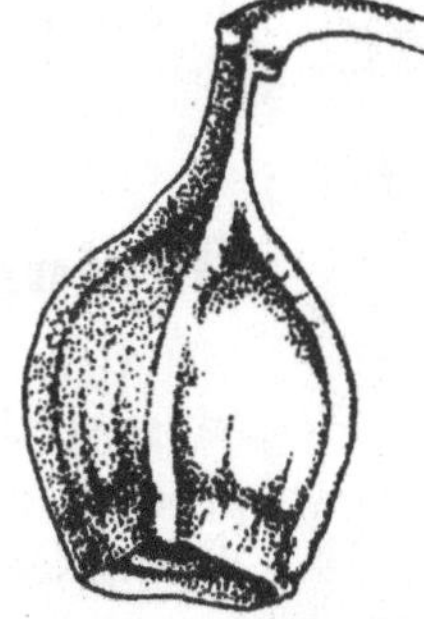

*Forrest's marlock (*E. forrestiana*).*

*Red flowering gum (*E. ficifolia*).*

Fruits of Eucalyptus *species.*

Chapter 2

Extracting the seed

The table **Treatment of fruits for seed germination,** at the end of this chapter, gives an overview of how to treat five main fruit types and a variety of flower heads. Details of the extraction and storage processes are described below.

Drying the seed cases

Most seed cases release their seed by a simple drying process in a warm, airy place. Follow these steps for drying seed cases in warm, sunny weather.

1. Spread seed cases out thinly on newspaper, a tarpaulin or sheets of black plastic.
2. Leave in the sun or a well-ventilated place like a verandah or shearing-shed floor.
3. Protect from rodents and ants.
4. Turn the seed cases regularly.
5. When thoroughly dry (usually 1–3 days), shake or tumble the seed cases to remove every last seed.

In cooler weather, dry seed cases as follows.

1. Under cover, spread seed cases out thinly on an improvised wire-netting rack with a tarpaulin hung beneath the wire to catch the seed (see illustration). Indoors, place paper or cloth bags containing seed cases on a windowsill or any other warm position, or spread seed cases out on a wooden tray (don't use

metal trays as the metal may heat to a temperature that damages the seed). Turn the seed cases regularly and protect from ants and rodents.

2. When completely dry (usually 1–3 days, depending on temperature and humidity), shake the seed cases to remove the seed at the bottom of each case. This seed is usually the most viable.

Mesh rack for drying seed cases in cooler weather.

When the windowsills of our house are strewn with paper bags and wooden bowls of assorted cones, nuts, pods and flower heads, we enjoy a lovely, warm squirrel feeling as we tap, shake and admire the beauty of each unique seed receptacle. Every tiny seed with the potential to burst into life...

Getting every last seed

Since the seed at the bottom of the capsule is often the most fertile, it pays to extract every last seed. Most seed cases respond to one of the following methods.

- Using a piece of sheeting to catch the seed, shake the seed cases or tap them against a firm surface.
- Spread seed cases on a piece of sheeting and beat them with a green branch.
- Put the seed cases into an ice-cream container or any container with a lid, and shake vigorously.
- If the seed cases are still attached to small branches, beat them onto a piece of sheeting or a tarpaulin.
- For large quantities, place in a concrete mixer, along with blocks of wood, and rotate.

Seed cases that need help: banksias, hakeas and grevilleas

Banksias have evolved with a bushfire survival factor built into their seed-release pattern. So this bushfire trigger needs to be copied to extract seed from these unique plants. Here is the first method.

1. Place the cones in a small open fire or barbecue and allow them to catch alight all over. When most of the follicles have split open, use tongs to remove the cones.
2. Plunge the cones into a bucket of cold water to extinguish the flames and to open more follicles. Now remove the winged seeds (two per follicle), using tweezers. A screwdriver can sometimes be used to lever open stubborn follicles, but take care not to damage the seed.
3. If any follicles remain closed, return the cones to the fire and repeat the process.

Alternatively, use this method.

1. Place the cones on a metal tray in the oven, one species per tray.
2. Leave at 120°C for 1 hour or 185°C for 30 minutes.
3. Tap out any loose seed.
4. Plunge cones into cold water, to split open stubborn follicles.
5. Remove winged seeds with tweezers.
6. Repeat the process if necessary.

Some people soak the cones in water for up to one week before giving the 'bushfire' treatment.

Hakea and grevillea seed that is difficult to extract may also be treated by either of these two methods.

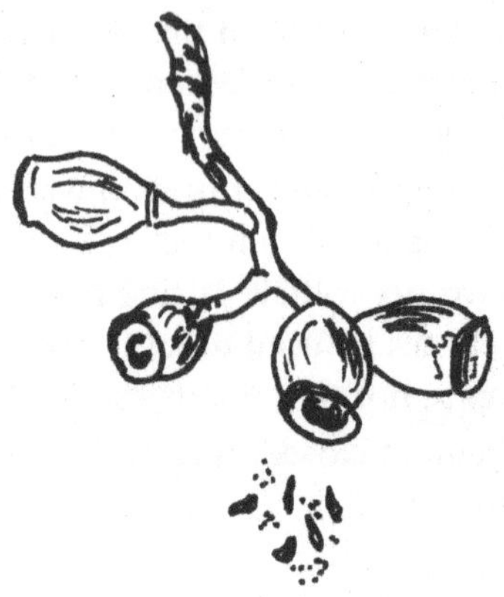

The darker-coloured fertile material is often only 10 – 20 per cent of the material shed from the seed case.

Cleaning the seed

Before you sow or store seed it needs to be separated from leaf, twig and seed-case material, but there is no need to be over-fussy, especially if you plan to sow soon. For example, it is not necessary to separate the infertile eucalypt seed from the fertile (the darker-coloured fertile material is often only 10–20 per cent of the material shed from the seed case). You simply make allowance for this when you sow. The following methods are adequate for most collectors.

- To dry and clean in the same operation, place the seed cases in a box with a wire mesh base, positioned over a seed-catching tray. The seed will fall through the mesh as it dries, and all that is required is a shake now and then, along with a turning-over of the seed cases.

- For seed cases that have already been dried, use a series of graded wire-mesh seed-sieves (or a kitchen colander or sieve) to separate the seed cases from the seed. Put the material into the sieve, cover, and shake energetically to ensure that all the seed comes out of every seed case.
- Use a stream of air (a light natural breeze, a hair dryer, an electric fan or a light blow from your mouth) to separate light waste material from the seed.

Seed cases spread to dry.

Checking for insect damage

The seed of native plants, as a concentrated food source, is very attractive to insects. Typically, an insect will lay its eggs inside the fruit, with the larvae (mainly moth and beetle) hatching to eat the soft fleshy part of the developing seed.

Plants such as kangaroo paw, acacias, hakeas, dryandras, banksias and those belonging to the iris and pea-flower families are particularly vulnerable. Warm, moist conditions favour the development of these larvae.

It is wise to inspect all seed carefully and to burn any seed showing evidence of insect damage.

Bay leaves and cloves will safely repel an insect invasion of your seed bank. Mothballs are likely to affect the viability of the seed and pose an unnecessary risk to your health.

Seed labelling and records

We always think we'll remember, but we don't! Label each bag (adhesive labels are useful) as you collect the seed cases, and include a leaf, flower or bark if you are unsure of the species. Keep a notebook in which you jot down collecting details. A typical label would read:

> 3.6.95
> Old Locksley School site
> *Eucalyptus microcarpa* (grey box)

Your own seed bank, along with a card system for records, is a very efficient way to ensure accuracy and good results in germination.

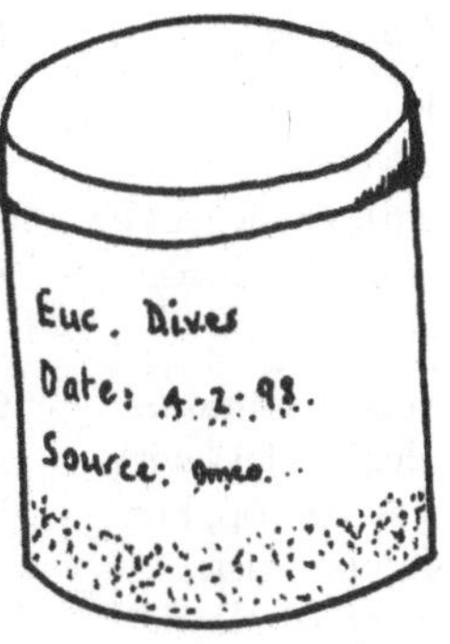

Labelled, sealed seed container.

Storing the seed

Your clean, dry, insect-free seed is now ready to be stored. Most Australian native seed stores quite well, but the seed from fleshy fruit (especially rainforest fruit) is best sown soon after collection.

Hot, humid conditions are difficult for the safe storage of seed. In these circumstances the best you can do is use a sealed container, pack it as full of dry seeds as possible, and store in a cool, dark place.

The following table sets out general methods for short-term and long-term storage; the table at the end of the chapter provides details.

Period	*Container*	*Place*
3–6 months	Paper, cloth bag or envelope, packed with bay leaves or cloves for insect control.	Cool, dry place, free from rodents, insects and mould.
6–12 months	Sealed container, ideally glass with a screw-top, but can be plastic, metal or plastic bag.	Cool, dark place in an insulated building. Temperature 10–25°C.
More than 12 months	Calico bag (along with calico bag of silica gel or other dessicant) in sealed container.	Refrigerator or coolroom. Temperature 0–6°C.

Seed viability

Seed must be fully mature to be viable, so select seed cases located on older wood and avoid picking green pods.

Correct storage is important for viability; however, most Australian native seed lasts for many years. Acacia and eucalypt seed can remain viable for amazing periods. But for best results, plan to sow seed within one year of collection.

Most seed should germinate within four weeks. If nothing has emerged after six weeks, pour boiling water over the seed bed to stimulate germination: it may have been stored in a place that was too hot and too dry for optimum germination.

Treatment of fruits for seed germination

As well as setting out specific details of the processes described in this chapter, the table on the following pages describes how to treat a large range of fruits for maximum seed germination.

Fruit type/ Family or species	*Description of fruit/ Extraction of seed*	*Appearance of seed/ Treatment*	*Storage of seed*	*Germination period & conditions*
PEA-LIKE PODS				
Acacia (wattle) *Albizia* (cape wattle) *Cassia* *Hardenbergia* *Kennedia* *Clianthus formosus* (Sturt desert pea)	Typical pea-like pods that split along two edges when ripe (mid-spring to end summer). Dry, shake, then sieve to separate pods from seeds. Microwave oven may be used to open pods. Set on DEFROST for 60 seconds.	Most have black or brown very hard-coated seeds. Pour almost boiling water over seeds and let them soak overnight, or nick seed coat with knife or razor blade.	Stores well for extended periods—68 years plus!	2—7 days after treatment. Hardenbergias, acacias and some kennedias vary widely in germination time; so try a second crop. Sow Sturt pea direct into ground.

Fruit type/ Family or species	*Description of fruit/ Extraction of seed*	*Appearance of seed/ Treatment*	*Storage of seed*	*Germination period & conditions*
FLESHY BERRIES				
Rainforest fruits	Will not tolerate drying and extraction.	Seed within colourful fleshy fruit. No treatment.	Will not store; sow on collection, in humus-rich soil.	1—3 days, at 30°C or over for northern species.
Pittosporum	Orange or yellow berries with tough leathery skin. Split into halves when ripe. Remove seed with knife and fork.	Mass of bright red seeds in a very sticky substance insoluble in water. Dry quickly. No treatment.	More viable when fresh.	3—12 weeks although some species may take up to four months.
Acmena (syn. *Eugenia*) e.g. lilly-pilly	Fleshy pale pink berries with crisp texture and skin. Remove outer pulp by cutting or breaking berries. Clean seeds with brush and water or soak berries in water for two days then put through sieve to separate seed. Dry quickly.	Single seed embedded in fleshy material of berry. No treatment.	Can be successfully stored if cleaned, sterilised and dried. Otherwise sow directly.	Up to 4 weeks.

Fruit type/ Family or species	*Description of fruit/ Extraction of seed*	*Appearance of seed/ Treatment*	*Storage of seed*	*Germination period & conditions*
FLESHY BERRIES *continued*				
Astroloma e.g. cranberry heath	Green or reddish-coloured fruit. Extract seed as for *Acmena*.	No treatment.	3—6 months.	Spread seeds on surface of any soil in autumn for good results.
Eremophila e.g. spotted emu bush	Largish berries that turn brownish when ripe and drop to the ground.	Very hard seed. Use smoke treatment.	Can be successfully stored.	Can be difficult to germinate. Very variable germination period.

Fruit type/ Family or species	*Description of fruit/ Extraction of seed*	*Appearance of seed/ Treatment*	*Storage of seed*	*Germination period & conditions*
FLESHY FRUIT WITH HARD STONE				
Macadamia	3 cm diameter globular fruit with hard green coat. Splits along side to expose hard-shelled brown nut. When less mature, peel to extract single brown stone, then dry.	Wash hard brown seed daily in clean water for 2 weeks, keeping seed moist between washes by covering with black polythene. Add macadamia husks to potting mix.	Sow seed as soon as possible.	Two weeks, at 25°C or over.
Elaeocarpus e.g. blue quandong (parasitic)	Bright blue globular fruit about 3 cm diameter. Remove flesh from single stone and dry. Wrinkled nuts found beneath tree.	Hard, pitted stone enclosing kernel (the nut or seed). Crack stone to assist seed's germination.	Store seed in its shell.	Use couch grass as intermediate host.

Fruit type/ Family or species	*Description of fruit/ Extraction of seed*	*Appearance of seed/ Treatment*	*Storage of seed*	*Germination period & conditions*
FLESHY FRUIT WITH HARD STONE				
Santalum e.g. Northern Sandalwood (parasitic)	Succulent purplish-blue edible fruit about 1 cm diameter. Drops from plant when mature. Remove flesh from single stone and dry. Smooth nuts found under tree.	Keep stone for 1 year, then crack shell and remove seed. Sterilise for 30 minutes in dilute bleach solution. Place in moist wood shavings in plastic bag. Keep cool and dark.	Must be stored for 1 year in shell, in order for seed to fully mature.	3 weeks plus. Plant partly germinated seed, two-thirds buried, over host species root, e.g. couch grass.
Ceratopetalum e.g. NSW Christmas bush	Ripe brick-red fruit falls naturally from plant. No cleaning or drying necessary. Nut-like structure within fruit.	Sow whole fruit, including sepals. Place stalk end of fruit down. Sow 3—4 per pot and discard weakest seedlings.	1—2 weeks only.	Slow unless very fresh. Add blood and bone to potting mix and earth, to speed growth.
Coprosma e.g. currant bush	Small globular red fleshy fruit, up to 1 cm diameter. Drop when mature.	Sow whole fruit. No cleaning or drying necessary.	More viable when fresh.	Up to 4 weeks.

Fruit type/ Family or species	*Description of fruit/ Extraction of seed*	*Appearance of seed/ Treatment*	*Storage of seed*	*Germination period & conditions*
WINGED SEED				
Hakea (needle bush)	Nut-like woody fruit splits down one side to release two light papery winged seeds. Pick when mature and place in paper bag in warm place. Seed released in 2—3 weeks. If not, lightly burn or put in oven.	Papery wings enable seed to blow up to 3 km. Nick very hard coats or soak in almost boiling water. Use smoke method for *Hakea corymbosa* (see pages 48—50).	Germination very high with freshly extracted seed.	2—5 weeks. Susceptible to damping off, so avoid sowing or transplanting during humid weather.
Banksia (honeysuckle)	In most species, partly embedded follicles split down one side, but only after treatment mimicking bushfire. Light burning in an open fire or heating in an oven usually splits follicles.	Usually two black thin-winged seeds in each follicle, separated by woody divider. Use tweezers to remove seeds from follicles.	Germination very high with freshly extracted seed.	2—6 weeks. Susceptible to fungal conditions.
Allocasuarina, Casuarina (she-oak, buloke)	Place woody cones in paper bag in warm place for about 1 week. This will usually release seeds through small valves.	Small winged seeds.	Can be stored, but more viable fresh. Best sown less than 7 days or over 3 months old.	5—21 days, preferably in summer. Easy to germinate.

Fruit type/ Family or species	*Description of fruit/ Extraction of seed*	*Appearance of seed/ Treatment*	*Storage of seed*	*Germination period & conditions*
WINGED SEED *continued*				
Telopea e.g. NSW waratah	Keep brown pods in a well-ventilated area. Seed will be released as follicle splits longitudinally.	Tightly packed yellow winged seeds. Very susceptible to damping off; take extra care.	Preferably only 1 week; max. 6 months. 2 years if refrigerated.	14 days plus. Slow unless very fresh. Susceptible to fungal disease.
Nuytsia e.g. WA Christmas tree (parasitic)	Three-cornered fruit opens when mature, dry and papery, about March. Watch carefully or tie cloth bag around fruit, as it sheds suddenly.	Each follicle contains single winged seed. Place in pot with grass species, e.g. couch, as intermediate host.	Preferably 1—2 weeks. Maximum 6 months.	4 weeks, but slow to germinate unless very fresh.
Dryandra	Seeds in small hard woody follicles at base of old flower head. Freshly picked follicles open in warm conditions more readily than those stored for longer periods, so place into paper bag and keep warm. Failing this, lightly burn in fire or place in warm oven or pan. Remove seeds with tweezers.	Two winged seeds in each follicle.	Seed needs to be fresh for good results.	High germination rates if seed is very fresh. Susceptible to fungal conditions.

Fruit type/ Family or species	*Description of fruit/ Extraction of seed*	*Appearance of seed/ Treatment*	*Storage of seed*	*Germination period & conditions*
WINGED SEED *continued*				
Grevillea (spider flower)	Place mature pods in paper bag, in warm dry place. 1—2 seeds per light woody pod is usual. As seed tends to explode on ripening, pick pods slightly immature or tie cloth bag around ripening pod.	Seed may be large and winged, or small with no wing. Increased germination rate if seed is soaked in water or lightly nicked or scratched.	More viable when fresh, but can be stored for up to 6 months.	1—8 weeks. Average 3 weeks in warm weather. *Grevillea banksii* and *G. robusta* germinate very well.
Isopogon e.g. rose cone bush	Cut off oldest flower heads. To release seed, break up small dry cone or keep cone in warm place for 1—2 weeks, then tap cone lightly and seed will fall out. A little heat may be applied if necessary.	A few fertile seeds to each flower head. Seed is dandelion-like; nut is covered with short stiff hairs. Use smoke method for improved germination.	Store in very dry place to avoid fungal damage.	2—3 weeks. Easy to germinate. Can be sown directly with very good results.

Fruit type/ Family or species	*Description of fruit/ Extraction of seed*	*Appearance of seed/ Treatment*	*Storage of seed*	*Germination period & conditions*
FINE SEED IN HARD WOODY CAPSULE				
Eucalyptus (gums, etc.) *Melaleuca* (paperbark) *Callistemon* (bottlebrush) *Calothamnus* (net bush)	Select oldest unopened seed cases, located on the oldest wood—usually over 12 months old and brown to grey in colour. Place mature capsules in paper or cloth bag and leave in warm dry place. Shake and tap seed cases vigorously to release all seed from capsules, as seed in bottom is most fertile.	Large quantities of very small seed, like ground pepper. Eucalypts have 80% light brown infertile seed, 20% dark brown to black fertile seed; sow thickly. No treatment, except eucalypts from cold climates; to break dormancy, store 6—8 weeks at 4°C in moist sand-peat mix.	11 years plus.	*Eucalyptus* 7—14 days. *Melaleuca, Callistemon* and *Calothamnus* 14—21 days. Easy to germinate.
Leptospermum (tea-tree)	Hard woody capsules split open along a number of sides to release seed.	Very fine seed. No treatment.	5—20 years in sealed container at 1—5°C.	14—21 days.

Fruit type/ Family or species	*Description of fruit/ Extraction of seed*	*Appearance of seed/ Treatment*	*Storage of seed*	*Germination period & conditions*
FINE SEED IN HARD WOODY CAPSULE *continued*				
Kunzea	Woody to fleshy to succulent edible fruit release seed rapidly at maturity, while still on tree. Cover with cloth bag to ensure collection.	Very fine seed. Pour boiling water over seeds and leave to soak overnight.	Stores well.	Easy to germinate.
Angophora (apple box)	Woody capsules release seed rapidly at maturity, while still on tree. Cover with cloth bag to ensure collection.	Three flat oval seeds per capsule.	More viable when fresh, but can be stored up to 6 months.	Provide sun, not much moisture, and protection from cold winds. Susceptible to fungal attack.

Fruit type/ Family or species	*Description of fruit/ Extraction of seed*	*Appearance of seed/ Treatment*	*Storage of seed*	*Germination period & conditions*
OTHER FLOWER HEADS				
Patersonia (native iris)	Papery seed capsules split to release seeds as they dry out on the plant. Cut carefully to minimise seed spillage.	Remove seed coat for excellent germination results.	More viable when fresh.	14—21 days. Easy to germinate.
Blandfordia (Christmas bells)	Narrow, elongated 3-angled capsules.	No treatment needed.	More viable when fresh.	14—21 days. Easy to germinate.
Boronia	Each capsule consists of 4—5 parts, each holding a seed. Tie cloth bag around mature flower to catch shiny black seeds as they explode from capsule.	Most western species germinate easily; eastern species, and their close relatives *Crowea* and *Eriostemon*, require treatment. Use dry heat or nick seed before hanging in running water for 7—14 days, or light a fire over seed bed, burn 5 minutes, cool, then water.		Very variable.
B. megastigma (brown boronia)	As for *Boronia*.	Store seed in sand-peat mix in refrigerator for 3 weeks before planting. Do not freeze.		Variable.

Fruit type/ Family or species	*Description of fruit/ Extraction of seed*	*Appearance of seed/ Treatment*	*Storage of seed*	*Germination period & conditions*
OTHER FLOWER HEADS *continued*				
Anigozanthos (kangaroo paw)	Pick flower head as colour fades and it becomes brittle and dry. Most capsules release seed when placed in paper bag in the sun. Position flower heads to hang upside down.	Crack tough capsules with rolling pin to release seeds (3 per capsule). No other treatment.	Up to 6 months.	14—21 days.
Hibiscus	When ripe, capsule turns brown and splits open. Shake to extract all the seed.	Seed that is chipped, nicked or pricked usually germinates more easily.	Stores well.	Easy to germinate.
Asteraceae family (daisies)	Pick heads when centre becomes loose and daisies are perfectly dry. Place in paper bags.	Light feathery seed. No treatment.	Store in very dry place to avoid fungal damage. Check for caterpillars.	3—7 days.

Fruit type/ Family or species	*Description of fruit/ Extraction of seed*	*Appearance of seed/ Treatment*	*Storage of seed*	*Germination period & conditions*
OTHER FLOWER HEADS *continued*				
Helichrysum (everlastings)	Must be collected when flower centre loosens, for seed to be mature.	Lightly feathery seed. No treatment.	Up to 3 years.	3 days—3 weeks. Best sown directly into moist raked outdoor seed bed. Scatter seed and tread in lightly.
Thryptomene	Tie a paper bag around flower to collect seed from capsules when they mature and shed.	Success has been achieved by scattering dry seed capsules on sandy soil as they mature. Smoke, heat or abrasion treatment can be tried to improve germination.	1—2 weeks best; up to 6 months.	Very slow to germinate unless very fresh. May take 12 months. Difficult to germinate even with treatment.
Clematis (travellers joy, white beard)	Attractive clusters of feathery fruit.	Plumed seed. Germinate at 10—25°C.	Only 1—2 weeks.	3—4 weeks. Very slow unless very fresh.

Fruit type/ Family or species	*Description of fruit/ Extraction of seed*	*Appearance of seed/ Treatment*	*Storage of seed*	*Germination period & conditions*
OTHER FLOWER HEADS *continued*				
Actinotus e.g. NSW flannel flower	Daisy-like flower heads rest in soft flannel-like leafy structures.	Small dense mature heads contain tightly packed seed. Use smoke method.	Only 1—2 weeks.	7 days—1 year. Very slow unless very fresh. Cover lightly with sand.
Chamelaucium e.g. Geraldton wax	Flower head dries to form capsule with many seeds.	Fine seed.	More viable when fresh.	Up to 4 weeks.
Conospermum (smoke-bush)	Large number of flowers but few fertile seeds, unless conditions are very favourable. Place bag over furry grey flower to safeguard single seed in conical fruit. Fruit must be fully mature, which takes some time.	Seed in small cone-shaped fruit. Use smoke method for improved germination.	Up to 6 months.	Easy to germinate fresh viable seed.

*Blackwood (*Acacia melanoxylon*), showing seed pod.*

Chapter 3

Seed needing special treatment before sowing

How dormancy is broken

Most seed from Australian plants is soft and will germinate easily when placed in a warm, moist environment. This 'soft' seed can be divided into two broad groups.

- **Fine seed**, for example from eucalypts, callistemons, calothamnus, tea-trees, melaleucas.
- **Larger seed**, for example from grevilleas, angophoras, banksias, hakeas and boronias.

There are some species, however, that produce very tough, hard-coated seed, and others that require special treatment in order to break dormancy. These plants have evolved to withstand the extremes of drought, bushfire, floods or snowy winters. Their seeds have developed characteristics that may require one of the following.

- Baking – the drought effect.
- Scorching or smoking – the bushfire effect.
- Repeated wetting – the rainy season or flood effect.
- Moist chilling – the alpine effect.

Dormancy delays germination for a period ranging from a couple of months to many years. This time of waiting ensures the plant's survival in the wild by allowing germination to occur only when conditions are ideal.

A bushfire burns away plant undergrowth, produces a nutrient-rich seed bed and is often followed by a thunderstorm. In addition the bushfire scorches all the hard-coated seed, making it permeable to moisture, so that the first rain after the bushfire results in a very large germination of acacias and other pea-like plants in particular. These quick-growing species help hold the soil together, enrich the earth with nitrogen via nodules on their root structures, and form a protective base from which other plants can grow.

Treating hard-coated seed and dormant embryos

Each method described below acts as a trigger to germination and imitates a climatic situation.

Baking

Place seeds in glass, ceramic or polystyrene containers in a domestic microwave oven. Set the timer in the range 30 seconds to 4 minutes, depending on the moisture content and the size of the seed. Larger moist seed will need longer than small dry seed. Acacia seed usually requires about 2 minutes. Experiment with small quantities to avoid wastage.

Scorching

Plant seeds as described in Chapter 4, then cover with a thin layer of dry twigs and leaves, straw or shredded paper. Set alight and keep burning for about 5 minutes. The dry heat will crack the seed coat and so enable the seeds to absorb the moisture necessary for germination. Allow the soil to cool, water well and place the trays in a position that will receive morning sun only, and protection from wind.

Eastern species of *Eriostemon* (wax flower) and *Boronia* require this type of dry heat treatment.

Cutting, abrading or peeling

For larger seeds, the hard seed coat can be cut, nicked or pricked, using a very sharp knife, a razorblade or a needle; however, care must be taken not to nick too deep or to make the cut too large.

Alternatively, file a nick in each seed until white shows through. This is a very slow and tedious method, but is quite effective, especially for seeds such as Sturt desert pea.

Scratching the seed coverings between two sheets of medium to coarse sandpaper is an efficient means of abrading the seed coats. Your aim is to allow water to pass through – but care must be taken to protect the soft interior. Species of *Verticordia* (feather flower) are best treated this way.

Some seeds respond well to being peeled.

Soaking in near-boiling water

The natural heating of a fire can be quickly and easily mimicked by placing seeds in a kitchen basin, pouring plenty of near-boiling water over them and allowing them to stand overnight. This process should soften the hard coat, dissolve the waxy covering and enable water to enter and swell the seed.

Some seeds are so tough they may require repeated soakings. When ready to sow they are swollen and soft enough to be broken with a fingernail. One treatment is sufficient for most acacias.

After soaking, drain the seed and wash it in clean cold water to remove any gelatinous substance. Discard any seed that floats, as this seed is usually infertile or inferior.

The seed can be sown in its soft wet state; however, fungal attack may be a problem if the seed is not sown straight away. Alternatively, the seed can be dried and sown later, provided the drying is done quickly and carefully.

A similar effect can be achieved by simply pouring boiling water over seed sown in a seed tray.

Soaking in running water

The aim is to imitate a rainy season or flood, during which water leaches out the chemicals that inhibit germination.

It is a good idea to nick the seeds or soak them in hot water before this treatment, but it is not always necessary.

Wrap the seeds in a muslin bag and tie the bag so that the seeds hang beneath running water for 7–14 days. This prolonged washing will break the dormancy.

Sowing seed in warm weather

Some seed responds well to sowing at the onset of warm weather, particularly in spring; for example *Persoonia*, *Correa*, *Grevillea*, *Boronia*, *Crowea* and *Eriostemon*.

Moist chilling

This method mimics seeds lying on the ground beneath snow during winter, then germinating with the onset of warm spring weather.

Seeds produced by plants growing in very cold or alpine areas are the most receptive to moist chilling. Eucalypts from the high country (for example alpine ash or snow gum) require this treatment.

Place seeds in damp sand or moist peat moss, wrap in plastic and secure package with rubber bands to keep it airtight. Alternatively, sow seed in a seed tray, moisten, then cover with plastic and seal to prevent drying. Store in the bottom of a refrigerator (not freezer) for 3–12 weeks.

The seed will usually sprout 3–14 days after removal from the refrigerator, if placed in a warm sheltered position.

Dark storage

This method imitates conditions where seed is buried beneath a deep layer of leaf litter on the forest floor, usually during a dry spell. Store your seed in a dry dark place for 3–6 months, to give the dormant embryos time to develop before sowing and germination.

Smoking

Recent research at Kings Park and Botanic Garden in Perth, Western Australia, has developed a new approach for the reliable germination of many species of Australian native seed, including species that are difficult to germinate – using conventional methods. A lead by South African scientists sparked this research.

The smoke process is simple, very effective, and of enormous horticultural importance since it offers new hope in the conservation of rare and endangered species.

The beneficial effects of bushfire in the germination of seed are well known, and were originally thought to be largely the result of the heat and ash from the fire.

Heat releases ethylene from the soil, so triggering terrestial orchids to flower; heat chars the woody seed cones of banksias, which then release their winged seed, once the fire has passed; heat cracks the hard seed coats of legumes such as *Hardenbergia*, *Acacia*, *Kennedia* and *Hovea* , so that when the rains come, germination can take place. In addition, fire reduces the competition for light and enriches the nutrients available to germinating seeds.

Smoke, with its complexity of over 4000 chemicals, had never before been considered in Australia as the sole agent in breaking seed dormancy. To date, this research has been applied successfully to over 400 species of Australian native plants; including trees, scrubs, herbs and annuals.

Research on Middle Island (south-western Western Australia) demonstrates how dependent some plants are upon fire. Seeds lay dormant on the island, waiting for smoke and/or heat of a fire to trigger their germination. And they waited for 170 years!

Smoke, a natural pesticide effect

It has been suggested that the application of aerosol smoke to seeds may offer some protection against predation and micro-

bial attack – making seed unpalatable to birds, animals and insects, as well as resistant to attack by bacteria. What a wonderful natural pesticide!

Some of the genera most suited to the smoke method include *Verticordia*, *Conospermum*, *Epacris*, *Eriostemon*, *Hybanthus*, *Leschenaultia*, *Pimelea*, *Stirlingia*, *Geleznowia*, *Actinotus*, *Hibbertia*, *Grevillea*, *Hakea*, *Calytrix*, *Blancoa* and *Stylidium*. Not only does smoke promote germination, it also assists earlier and more uniform germination, and young plants that are stronger and healthier. Smoking offers an alternative to controlled burning for the germination of seeds normally dependent upon fire.

The West Australian research shows that germination can be increased by as much as 50 times for some species. In other species, germination of viable seed can be 100 per cent. Economically, the smoke method is an enormous breakthrough. It is the first reliable method for the propagation of many Australian plants grown specifically for the cut flower market. In addition, this new smoke technology will ensure that degraded land (for example, mining sites) can be restored with a richer diversity of plants. Dormant seeds can even be stimulated in their natural habitat, speeding up revegetation.

How does smoke get to the seed buried beneath the leaf litter?

After an artificial smoking (or bushfire), smoke settles in the soil and remains there undisturbed until rain washes the smoke through the soil, releasing the smoke chemicals to the seed.

When is the best time to smoke the seed?

For best germination combine smoke with ideal seasonal temperature and age of seed. Smoke is the signal the seed needs to tell it that a bushfire has occurred and that conditions are now ideal for germination.

Autumn to early winter is the best season to smoke your seed in southern Australia. This ensures that there is adequate time for the plant to establish itself before the long dry summer period. For other regions, imitate Nature as closely as possible.

What are the 3 most common methods of making and using smoke?

(i) Pure cool smoke

To smoke seed (for up to one hour) you will need the following.

- A 100 litre metal combustion drum, with an air inlet hole in the bottom and an outlet in the lid.
- A small tent or tent-like structure (sealed at the bottom to minimise leakage) to contain the smoke. The tent can be fitted with up to 3 levels of shelving, with 30 cm between each shelf, to allow good smoke flow throughout.
- Hose or flexible piping connecting the tent with the outlet in the lid of the drum.
- A small pump (for example, an air mattress pump) to push the smoke from the drum through the outlet hole in the lid.
- A mixture of green and dry native plant foliage and twigs, of any variety.
- Seed, or trays of sown seed.

The method is simple.

1. Place the seed (spread out in a single layer in trays) or trays of sown seed in the tent.
2. Light the foliage in the drum and adjust the air flow on the air pump, so that it burns but does not flame.
3. Direct the smoke from the drum into the tent via the connecting hose or pipe.
4. Smoke the seed for about one hour.

5. Remove the seed (or trays of sown seed) from the tent. With the trays, you will notice a brown staining on the surface of the soil, and a definite smell of smoke lasting for 6–8 days.
6. Using rain water, moisten the trays carefully for the first week in particular, so that the chemicals deposited in the smoking process are not washed away too rapidly. Smoke is highly water soluble.

(ii) Smoke dissolved in water

Seed can be soaked in smoked water to improve the rate of germination. Alternatively, seed can be sown then watered with concentrated smoked water. This will leave a light brown stain. To produce smoked water you will need a number of items.

'Smoke tent' method of smoking seed.

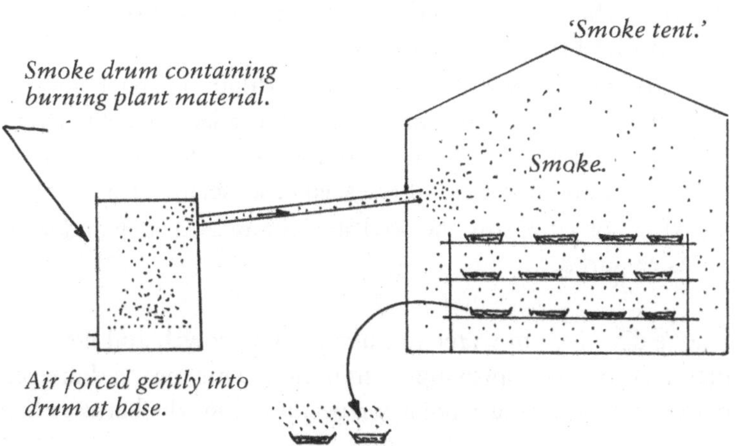

- A 100 litre metal combustion drum, with an air-inlet hole in the bottom and an outlet in the lid.
- A 20–30 litre drum, filled with water, through which the smoke is drawn.
- One vacuum cleaner.
- A 20–30 litre drum (which is empty), to stop water being sucked back into the vacuum cleaner.
- Hose or flexible piping connecting the 100 litre drum to the two 20–30 litre drums.
- A mixture of green and dry native foliage and twigs, of any variety.

Use the following method.

1. Light the foliage in the drum and adjust the air flow so that it burns but does not flame.
2. Direct the smoke from the combustion drum into the water-filled drum via the connecting hose or pipe.
3. Allow the smoke to bubble through the water for about one hour.
4. Apply this concentrated smoke water to sown trays at the rate of 1 litre per square metre.
5. If you are going to soak your seed, dilute one part smoked water with nine parts rain water. Most seed benefits from an overnight soak. Between 6–24 hours (depending upon the size and hardness of the seed case) seems ideal.
6. After soaking, sow the seed straight away or dry and sow as required.

Smoke dissolved in water stimulates root growth and development, as well as improving germination. This means that even plants not requiring smoke for germination, do better when smoked.

Making smoked water.

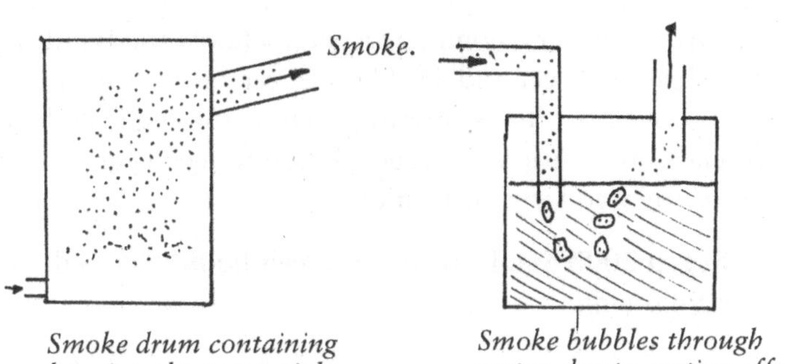

Smoke drum containing burning plant material.

Smoke bubbles through water, due to suction effect.

(iii) REGEN 2000 ®

A synthesised smoke product has been developed by an enterprising Australian company. The original research was conducted under the technical guidance of scientists at Kings Park and Botanic Garden, Perth, Western Australia, who also trialled Regen 2000 Direct.

Regen 2000 is prepared by heating hardwood sawdust, to the point of decomposition. The smoke is then 'captured' on water, and the water/smoke combination recycled until the desired concentration is reached. It is 100 per cent natural.

This concentrated smoke product can be used to smoke seed trays, seeds or bushland soil, with remarkable results in terms of germination.

Schools, Landcare groups, nurseries and gardening enthusiasts find the process so simple and effective that they are becoming more adventurous in their choice of seed to propagate. Featherflowers; triggerplants; native lilies, violets, rushes and heaths; cottonheads; smokebushes; hakeas and grevilleas – all these germinate very well using Regen 2000.

There are 3 products: Regen 2000 Smokemaster, a green liquid; Regen 2000 Direct, a red liquid; and Regen 2000 Seed Starter, a dry form.

Smokemaster treats the seed used by nurseries, the producers of native cutflowers, home gardeners, schools and Landcare groups; whereas Direct and Seed Starter tend to be used in the restoration of larger areas of land, such as mining, Landcare and special conservation projects, where the seed is already in the soil or sown in large quantities.

To use Regen 2000 Smokemaster, a green liquid, you will need the following:

- Regen 2000 Smokemaster
- Seed or trays of sown seed.
- Water.

The method is simple.

1. Depending on the size of the seed, mix the appropriate amount of liquid – at the rate of 100 ml of Smokemaster to 1 litre of water. Using this dilute solution, soak your seed for 6–24 hours. The treated seed is then dried and broadcast, or sown directly into seed trays.
2. For trays sown with seed, spray the surface of the soil with undiluted Smokemaster. 100 ml will cover 1 square metre. Now water sparingly for 6–10 days. Too much water will wash the Smokemaster through the soil too rapidly, whereas careful watering will take the smoke product to the waiting seed, where it will trigger germination over the 4–6 weeks it takes for germination to take place.

To use Regen 2000 Direct, a red liquid, you will need the following:

- Regen 2000 Direct
- A boom or aerial spray unit.
- An area of land containing a natural seed bank, or over which untreated seed has been broadcast.

The method is simple.

1. This highly concentrated smoke water is designed to be sprayed, undiluted, onto the surface of the soil. For best results, 100 ml will be needed to cover 1 square metre.
2. Rain (autumn or early winter rains in southern Australia) will wash the Regen 2000 Direct to the seed, where it will stimulate germination.

Using Regen 2000 Seed Starter, a dry form:

Seed Starter is the most recent development of this unique product. Whereas Smokemaster and Direct are applied in solution with water, Seed Starter is dry. This makes it much easier and cheaper to apply to large areas.

Being the consistency of vermiculite, it will mix easily with seed broadcast from the air or via a seeding machine. So, seeding and smoking can now be achieved in one simple operation. You will need the following.

- Regen 2000 Seed Starter
- A means of broadcasting the product:
  by hand for small areas,
  by Seeder for large areas, and
  by helicopter for extensive rugged terrain.
- An area of land containing a natural seed bank or over which seed and Seed Starter can be broadcast.

The method is very simple.

1. This small and highly concentrated smoke pellet is designed to fall onto the surface of the soil. For best results, 75 grams will be needed to cover 1 square metre.
2. Rain (autumn or early winter rains in southern Australia) will wash the Regen 2000 Seed Starter to the seed, where it will stimulate germination.

Australian genera which are responsive to smoke for germination under nursery or field conditions, compiled by Kings Park and Botanic Garden, Perth, include:

Acacia
Acanthocarpus
Acrotriche
Actinostrobus
Actinotus
Adenanthos
Agonis
Agrostocrinum
Allocasuarina
Alyxia
Amphipogon
Andersonia
Anigozanthos
Arthropodium
Astartea
Astroloma
Baeckea
Banksia
Billardiera
Blancoa
Boronia
Bossiaea
Brunonia
Burchardia
Bursaria
Caesia
Callitris
Calytrix
Chamaescilla
Chieranthera
Clematis
Cadonocarpus
Comesperma
Conospermum
Conostephium
Conostylis
Crassula
Cryptandra
Cyathochaeta
Dampiera
Desmocladus
Dianella

Diplolaena
Drosera
Epacris
Eriostemon
Eucalyptus
Exocarpus
Gahnia
Geleznowia
Georgiella
Gompholobium
Gonocarpus
Grevillea
Gyrostemon
Haemodorum
Hakea
Hemigenia
Hemiphora
Hibbertia
Hovea
Hyalosperma
Hybanthus
Hydrocotyle
Hypocalymma
Isopogan
Isotoma
Johnsonia
Kennedia
Lachnostachys
Lasiopetalum
Laxmannia
Lechenaultia
Leptomeria
Leptospermum
Leucopogon
Levenhookia
Lobelia
Lomandra
Loxocarya
Lysinema
Macropidia
Melaleuca
Mitrasacme
Myriocephalus
Neurachne
Opercularia
Orthrosanthus
Patersonia
Petrophile
Phyllanthus
Pimelea
Pityrodia
Platysace
Pomaderris
Poranthera
Ptilotus
Ricinocarpus
Rulingia
Scaevola
Siegfriedia
Sollya
Sowerbaea
Sphenotoma
Spryidium
Stackhousia
Stipa
Stirlingia

Stylidium
Tersonia
Tetraria
Tetrarrhena
Tetratheca
Thysanotus
Trachymene
Trichocline
Tripterococcus
Trymalium
Velleia
Verticordia
Waitzia
Xanthorrhoea
Xanthosia

Note
This list of smoke responsive genera does not indicate a positive response from all species within each genera. A positive response from one species does not guarantee a positive response from a related species. Many species remain untested, due to the incredible numbers involved. Perhaps you can help?

Summing up

Any Australian plant seed that does not germinate readily may have a very tough covering or a dormant embryo. Any of the above methods, or a combination of them, will help break this dormancy, and it is well worth experimenting with small batches of seed to see which method works best.

Smoke stimulates seed germination and offers new hope in the conservation of rare and endangered species. In addition, the smoke method is the first reliable method for the propagation of many plants grown specifically for the lucrative cut flower market.

Remember that new discoveries are being made all the time, so record your results. Perhaps you can help develop new methods of germinating Australian seed?

Chapter 4

Planting the seed

Seed, as the reproductive structure of the plant, consists of an embryo and a food store, surrounded and protected by an outer seed coat. Infinite in variety, size and shape, the seed on germination develops into a new plant; but it must have air, warmth and moisture to fulfil its role, which is to continue the species.

Best sowing times

Soil temperature is crucial to germination, so naturally germination time varies, depending on seasonal conditions.

An air temperature of about 20°C is considered suitable for germination, with 23°C being the ideal for most species. Tropical plants require slightly higher temperatures (23–30°C), but this can easily be achieved with a glasshouse, a sheet of glass or a warm verandah. Plants from alpine areas will germinate at 15–20°C.

Most species can be sown in either autumn or spring, but spring is usually the best season to sow seed.

Autumn sowing

If autumn is chosen, sow early and prick out seedlings before the onset of very cold weather, as the low temperatures will slow growth and may cause root rot.

Unless sown early, seedlings are often too fragile (that is, not woody enough) to survive the winter months.

Winter sowing

If seeds are sown during winter, the cold temperatures may slow down germination to the extent that the seeds may actually rot in the soil, or lie dormant and only germinate with the onset of spring. Fungus can also cause problems with winter-sown seed.

Spring sowing

From the end of August to October is the best time to sow most species, especially Western Australian plants and those susceptible to fungal attack. Germination will be quick and the seedlings will grow vigorously and easily catch up and pass those sown in autumn.

Summer sowing

If seed is sown in December or January, leave the pricking-out until the end of March, when the seedlings will be stronger and less likely to dry out. A mid-summer sowing will certainly ensure rapid germination, but it can be difficult to keep the soil moist.

Allocasuarinas and casuarinas respond best to summer sowing.

Preparation of containers and equipment

Any shallow container can be used to germinate seed, provided it is clean and has holes in the base to ensure good drainage. Parallel or near-parallel sides will help prevent root curl. Wooden or plastic seed trays, approximately 10cm deep and of any convenient size are suitable. Containers 40 cm square will provide space for the germination of hundreds of eucalypt seedlings.

Plastic margarine, yoghurt or ice-cream containers may also be used, along with cut-down milk cartons. New clay pots need to be first soaked in water for a couple of hours, then dried.

Many plant diseases are spread through contaminated soil, so hygiene is important when preparing containers and equipment. The cleanliness of your hands, the bench top, gardening gloves, trowels, wheelbarrow, spade and so on is important too: the seed you have collected is precious and it is very disappointing to lose a whole batch of tiny seedlings.

If plant disease is not a problem in your locality, simply rinse all equipment and containers in cold running water and dry in the sun. However, if fungal attack and other plant diseases are common, follow these steps.

1. Hose off any loose dirt.
2. Scrub in hot soapy water.
3. Soak in salty water for 5–10 minutes.
4. Rinse well.
5. Dry in the sun. Containers in particular will benefit from 2–3 days in the sunshine.

Alternatively, hose off loose dirt and sterilise with steam.

Preparation of soil mix

The soil mix is simply a structure in which to germinate the plant: a free-draining mix that must be able to hold some moisture.

Coarse sharp river sand is an excellent free-draining material, while humus and peat moss are able to absorb sufficient moisture to nourish the seedling.

A combination of river sand and humus or peat moss is perfect, for the sand does not pack tightly, a characteristic that allows particles of the humus or peat moss to sit comfortably between the grains. This ensures that the tiny plants receive adequate moisture, while at the same time their hair-like roots can grow easily between the grains in a soil mix that is free-draining.

Soil mixes to avoid include those that dry to a powdery dust, form a hard surface crust, become sticky when wet, or remain waterlogged. Any of the following mixes may be used.

- One part coarse sharp river sand to one part humus (decayed she-oak leaves are ideal).
- One part coarse sharp river sand to one part peat moss.
- One part coarse sharp river sand to one part loam.
- Three parts coarse sharp river sand to one part good quality topsoil (good in dry climates) and one part peat moss or humus.

Vermiculite, a sterile propagation mix obtainable from nurseries and garden supplies, swells to absorb moisture while allowing good drainage. Seeds can be propagated in this medium.

One of several suitable soil mixes:

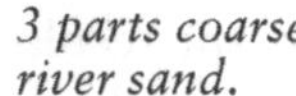

3 parts coarse river sand. *1 part peat moss.* *1 part topsoil.*

If you know or suspect there are disease problems, you can partly sterilise the soil mix in a kitchen oven. Normally this is not necessary. For small quantities, place the slightly moist mix in plastic oven bags, and heat to 60°C for up to 30 minutes. This gives enough heat to kill disease-causing agents without damaging soil structure, soil chemistry or other beneficial soil organisms. Alternatively, light a fire over the soil mix before sowing.

Now that your ingredients are ready, follow these steps before actually sowing the seed.

1. Sieve the separate parts of the soil mix through fine mesh. Any coarse material left in the sieve can be used in the bottom of pots to ensure good drainage.
2. Thoroughly mix together all the ingredients. A wheelbarrow is a suitable place to do this, using a spade.
3. Fill each seed tray or pot right to the top. The only exception to this rule is in the case of sowing acacias or other pea-like plants. These species have very vigorous root growth that pushes the seed up on germination, so leave plenty of space at the top and cover with a thicker layer of Vermiculite.
4. Level off the surface, tap the container on a bench or table to remove any air pockets, then press down the

soil mix lightly with something flat like the bottom of a drinking glass or a piece of smooth wood. The soil mix will now be about 1 cm from the rim of the container, which will leave ample space for the seed, its covering and for watering.

5. Water thoroughly before sowing seed. Stand the containers in a tray of water about half as deep as the mix, and leave until the surface shows a colour change (the result of moisture). Alternatively, use a fine spray to completely saturate the mix.

Sowing the seed

Seeds whether large or small should never be sown thickly, as crowding reduces air circulation and so creates ideal conditions for fungal disease. In addition, seed sown too densely tends to develop into seedlings with weak, spindly growth.

Fine seed

Fine seed (of eucalypts, callistemons, calothamnus, tea-trees and melaleucas) can be sown in any of the following ways.

- Sprinkle seed very lightly over the surface, using your fingers; however, do remember that seed of some genera, such as *Eucalyptus* and *Isopogon*, is accompanied by a quantity of infertile packing material, so that the number of seeds being planted may look more than it actually is.
- Use a salt or pepper shaker to sprinkle seeds lightly over the surface. This method is suitable for callistemons and tea-trees, which produce seed so fine it is almost like dust.

- Make a simple paper trough from which to sprinkle the seeds.
- Mix very fine seed with three times the volume of fine white sand. This will make it easier to sow evenly.

Cover the seed lightly, to no more than twice its thickness. This layer will protect the seed and help keep it moist. Use Vermiculite, sieved soil mix or fine washed sand (don't use beach sand). Avoid covering the seeds too deeply – a common reason why seeds fail to germinate, especially seed of the eucalypts. Aim to simply hide them from view.

Press down lightly and evenly with a piece of flat wood about the same size as the top of the container.

Water thoroughly. The best way to water freshly sown fine seed is to place the container in a tray or trough of water, with the water level as close to the top of the container as possible, and leave until the surface layer shows a colour change. With a Vermiculite layer the colour will change from a light gold to a darker shade when moist.

The colour will tell you when the seeds have received enough moisture and when they need their next watering, too! Overhead watering, even with a fine spray, runs the risk of 'digging up' the tiny seeds.

Larger seed

Follow these hints when sowing larger seed.

1. By hand, spread seeds on top of the soil mix, but take care to space them so that no seeds touch one another. By ensuring good air circulation, this method will discourage the spread of fungus.

2. Cover to a depth of twice the thickness of the seed, using sieved soil mix, sieved washed sand, Vermiculite, crushed she-oak needles, fine gravel, granite grit or fine blue metal. The heavier coverings will make overhead watering safer, whereas coverings such as crushed she-oak needles will help keep the seed bed moist and cool, especially in hot weather. Select your covering according to the season and the watering method.
3. Press down the covering material lightly and evenly, using a piece of flat wood about the same size as the top of the container.
4. Water thoroughly, either by placing each container in a tray or trough of water until the surface layer shows a colour change, or by overhead watering with a fine spray.

Larger seed with a good striking rate (seed of grevilleas, angophoras, banksias, hakeas, boronias and some acacias) can be sown directly into individual pots. If this method is used there is no pricking-out process.

During hot weather, a piece of hessian may be placed over the surface to help prevent drying out. This may be left on until the seeds germinate, which will vary from a few days to three months or longer! Most seeds will germinate within four weeks; however, some banksias may take up to four months.

Remember to *label* all your seed trays and containers with the date and type of seed, using small thin pieces of wood marked with indelible pencil, or plastic, metal or wooden tags with painted or waterproof Texta names.

Positions for seed containers

Raise seed containers up off the ground by placing them on a steel mesh frame or on slats of wood. Good drainage and air circulation help avoid fungal disease.

Protect the germinating seeds from attack by slugs and snails. Natural barriers using soot, lime, sawdust, grit, eggshells

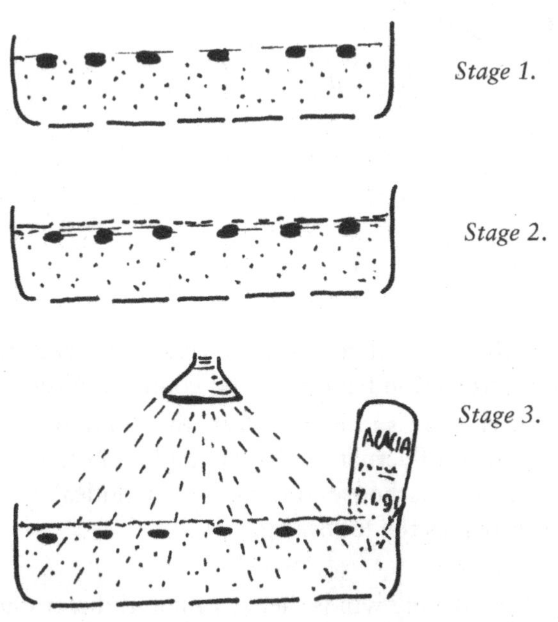

Seed planting.

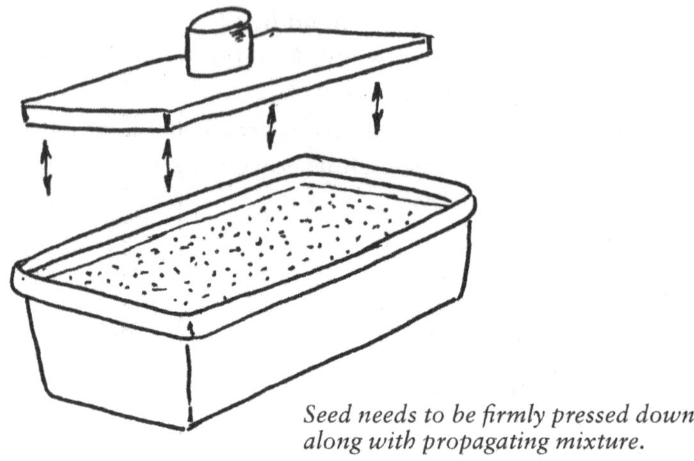

Seed needs to be firmly pressed down, along with propagating mixture.

or wood ash are effective in deterring these creatures. Seed trays will also require protection from pets and young children.

Germination is more successful when the containers are exposed to the natural fluctuations of day and night temperatures. For this reason glasshouse conditions are not ideal. Select a position that provides the following.

- Protection from drying winds, heavy rain and direct midday sun.
- Gentle light (semi-shade, that is, 50–70 per cent shade) that mimics conditions on the forest floor. An overshaded area tends to produce weak seedlings susceptible

to disease. Select such areas as: beneath an evergreen tree like a eucalypt; beneath shrubs that will cast dappled shade throughout the day; a shade house with 60 per cent shade; or a sunny room or verandah with slatted blinds.

- Airy conditions to avoid fungal disease.
- A warm (not hot) aspect, receiving early morning rather than midday or late sun. In most districts a protected area of the garden is warm enough for most autumn and spring sowings.
- In cold regions and for winter sowings, additional warmth. A glasshouse or propagation box can provide this; however, it is wise to keep a check on the temperature with a thermometer, as overheating will kill seedlings. A propagation box can be a very simple affair, for example a box with a sheet of glass or clear plastic as a lid. Shadecloth can be used when the weather warms up.

Watering

Water is crucial to the germination process, so the soil mix must not be allowed to dry out. It must be kept moist at all times, but not wet.

Water once or twice daily, three to four times a day in hot weather. A fine overhead spray is all right for larger seeds, but watering from below is better for very small seed, as tiny seedlings are easily damaged by overhead watering or rain.

Watering from below is also better for avoiding the group of fungal diseases collectively described as damping off.

Watering from below is relatively simple. Place your seed trays or containers in a tray, basin or trough of water so that the water level reaches about halfway up the containers.

Leave them standing in this position for about one month after germination. Keep the water level stable to ensure the sowing mix is always kept moist. Plastic bags may be placed over the seed trays or containers to help maintain warmth and moisture levels; however, keep a careful watch for fungal problems if you use plastic in this way. Dappled sunlight, cuts in the plastic bags and a soil mix that contains a high level of coarse sharp river sand will all help reduce fungal attack.

Hard water can result in poor germination, so use rainwater whenever possible.

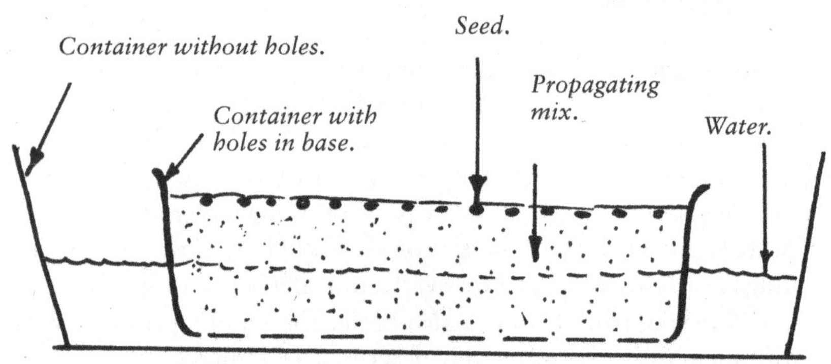

Watering from below.

Fertiliser

It is not necessary to add fertiliser to the soil mix used to germinate Australian native plants.

Failure to germinate

If nothing has germinated after 8–12 weeks, pour boiling water over the seed bed to stimulate germination.

If there is still no response, leave the pots to dry out. Perhaps the spring was too hot or the autumn too cold? Leave them in a dry state until the following season, then slot them into your new germination program, when conditions may be more favourable. Quite a few species that are difficult to germinate will respond the second time round.

Seed that has been stored in conditions that are too hot or too dry often takes a long time to germinate. In addition, older seed usually takes more time than freshly gathered seed.

When sowing seeds of acacias, hardenbergias, kennedias and other pea-like plants, always try for a second crop, especially if the first strike was disappointing. Seed of the same species may show tremendous variation in the time taken for germination.

Seeds of pittosporum may take up to four months to germinate, so be patient!

Fungal diseases

Damping off is the term used to describe a group of fungal diseases spread in the soil and common in cold, wet conditions. The disease may attack at any of the following stages.

- The seed will rot before it has a chance to germinate. The seed stock itself may be blamed, when it is really a fungus that has destroyed a perfectly sound seed.
- At the very early stage of germination, before the tiny sprout has reached the surface, a fungus may strike and kill the plant.
- Young seedlings may be attacked at the junction of the root and the stem, so the top falls over and the plant dies. This stem weakness is the most noticeable form of damping off.

Root rot and stem rot cause the roots or lower stem to become soft and brown, causing stem weakness and death.

Leaf spots appear as brown spots on leaves. This usually slows growth. The plant may die.

To avoid damping off and other fungal diseases, follow these hints.

- Clean and sterilise all equipment and containers before sowing (see **Preparation of containers and equipment** in this chapter).
- Heat-sterilise soil mix if you suspect fungal problems (see **Preparation of soil mix** in this chapter).
- Use a fresh soil mix for each new batch of seed.
- Sow seed during spring or autumn when temperatures are less extreme.
- Allow morning sun to fall on seed trays.
- Ensure good air circulation around seedlings by not sowing seed too thickly.
- Water from the bottom up, to reduce moisture around the seedlings.
- Avoid overhead watering late in the day.
- Do not prick out or transplant seedlings in humid conditions.

Direct seeding

Sowing seed directly is particularly valuable when very large areas need to be treed, as it is low-cost and saves time. In addition it saves water: trees sown in this manner do not need to be watered through their first summer, as their root systems are usually very well developed. These young trees tend to be hardier and more vigorous than tube stock, especially if local species are sown.

The use of herbicides is unnecessary if the area can be prepared in two steps.

1. Graze heavily.
2. Lightly plough, or burn with a light quick fire to reduce grass and weed competition.

Seed must be sown into a moist seed bed and is best sown in early spring. It can be planted by two methods.

1. **By machine**, using either a commercial tree seeder such as the Hamilton Treeseeder (it sows a single line of seed), or an ordinary seed drill with chains or pieces of brush dragged behind the machine to lightly cover the seed.
2. **By hand**, using seed mixed with sawdust or sand to give it extra bulk. After scattering by hand, lightly rake the area or drag a hessian bag over the seed bed.

Survival of direct-sown seed is estimated to be 1–5 per cent, so plenty of seed (150–300 g/km) must be sown to achieve good results. Alternatively, sow at the rate of 200–300 g/ha for fine seed and 300–500 g/ha for larger seed. Remember that most wattle seed will need to be treated to soften the hard coat (see Chapter 3 for details).

Good quality fencing is needed to protect the young trees from sheep, cattle and rabbits.

Natural regeneration

Natural regeneration relies on the establishment of trees and shrubs using seed that has fallen naturally from trees in that particular area. It is an inexpensive and time-saving way of establishing excellent shelterbelts, using existing single or sparse trees as seed stock.

The key to success lies in the careful preparation of the seed bed before the natural fall of seed, and in having adequate fencing to protect the young trees from damage by sheep, cattle and rabbits.

The use of herbicides is unnecessary if the area to be planted is prepared in two steps as for **Direct seeding**. Burning is an excellent alternative in step 2, as it will help germinate any dormant seed lying on the surface, for example wattle seed.

When planning areas to be set aside for natural regeneration, remember that a eucalypt usually sheds its seed 1–3 tree heights downwind from itself, during summer when hot dry winds are blowing.

*Drooping she-oak (*Allocasuarina verticillata*) and fruit.*

Chapter 5

Transplanting and growing on

In order to give seedlings room to develop a strong bushy root system without damage or kinking, each one needs to be transplanted into an individual container (**pricked out**) at an early stage, when its roots are nearly the depth of the seed tray, and then (**grown on**) until it is ready to be planted out. Many trees fail to thrive and die prematurely as a result of a setback in root structure at this vital stage.

Generally, seedlings pricked out during spring can be planted out the following autumn and those transplanted during autumn, planted out in mid to late spring. However, callistemons, calothamnus, tea-trees and melaleucas, which produce particularly tiny seedlings, are best germinated in spring, transplanted in autumn and planted out in spring. Acacias and eucalypts are faster growing and produce more substantial seedlings that allow germination in early spring, transplanting in late spring and planting out the following autumn.

Time to prick out

On germination many species, for example the eucalypts, sprout two tiny 'leaves' that are not true leaves at all. These are followed by the plant's first then second pair of true leaves. It is at this stage, between the growth of

the first and second true leaves, that the seedling needs to be transplanted into an individual container. The seedling will be about 3–5 cm high, big enough to handle without damage to the plant.

Select a cool day, preferably overcast with no wind. Humid conditions should be avoided if fungal disease is a problem in your area.

Preparation of containers and equipment

Any small container may be used to grow on the seedling, provided it has drainage holes in the bottom and is about 3–5 cm diameter and 10–15 cm deep. However, tubes are ideal as they take less space, use less soil mix and allow the development of a particularly deep, strong root system. These may be rolled from wood veneer or plastic film and secured with rubber bands or staples. The ideal size is 4–5 cm diameter and 15 cm deep. Special plastic containers of this size are also available.

For the cleaning and sterilising of containers and equipment see Chapter 4.

Preparation of soil mix

For growing on the young seedlings you need a good friable soil, a mixture slightly heavier than the seed mix. A suitable mix is five parts coarse sharp river sand to three parts loam and four parts peat moss or humus. All ingredients must be sieved and mixed thoroughly before use.

See Chapter 4 for the sterilisation, preparation and watering of soil mixes.

The pricking-out process

It has been estimated that 90 per cent of young tree deaths can be traced to root damage and distortion at the pricking-out stage. Great care must be taken to ensure that each seedling has a straight root system, with as little damage and disturbance as possible. Here are the steps for successful pricking out.

1. Fill each tube with soil mix, right to the top.
2. Tap tube on a bench or table to remove any air pockets.
3. Stand all the tubes in a rack in a tray of water about half as deep as the tubes, and leave until the soil surface is moist.
4. Take each tube and, with the aid of a wooden spoon handle or something similar, poke a hole in the centre of the soil mix, nearly to the bottom.
5. Place a basin of dry soil mix on your work table, along with a basin of clean cool water.
6. Stand the container of tiny seedlings in water, to about half the depth of the container, and leave until the surface is moist.
7. Gently but firmly remove the seedlings from their container, in one clump. Tease out the roots if they have become tangled. Rest the clump on a flat plate.
8. Now remove a single seedling from the clump. Very carefully ease it away from the others, with your fingers holding the leaves, preferably the lower leaves. Do not pull it away by the stem, as the stem is easily bruised and this could kill the plant, while bruised leaves will recover or be replaced.
9. With the roots hanging free, cut off any turned or twisted roots, using a pair of scissors sterilised by boiling water or steam. If the root system is longer than the tube, trim it off to the tube length. Also trim any side root that looks too developed.

10. Dip the roots in the basin of water, to bring the roots together in one streamlined flow.
11. Sprinkle the roots with dry soil mix to weight them so that they will thread neatly into the hole in the tube.
12. Lower the roots into the hole, then with your other hand gently firm the soil around the seedling.
13. Tap the tube on the edge of the bench to settle the soil and remove air pockets. It may be necessary to add a little more soil mix to secure the seedling and have the soil within 1 cm of the top of the tube.
14. Place the tube in a rack and attach a label to identify the species.
15. When the rack is fully loaded, place it in a tray or tub of water with the water level as high as possible.
16. Remove from the water when the moisture has thoroughly soaked the tubes (this should not take long at all).

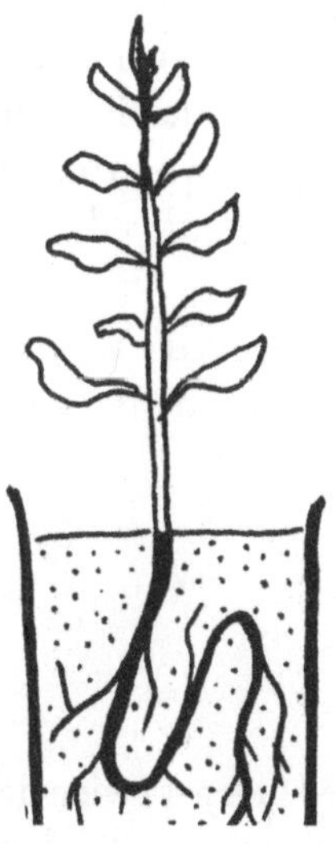

Poor plant development due to twisted roots.

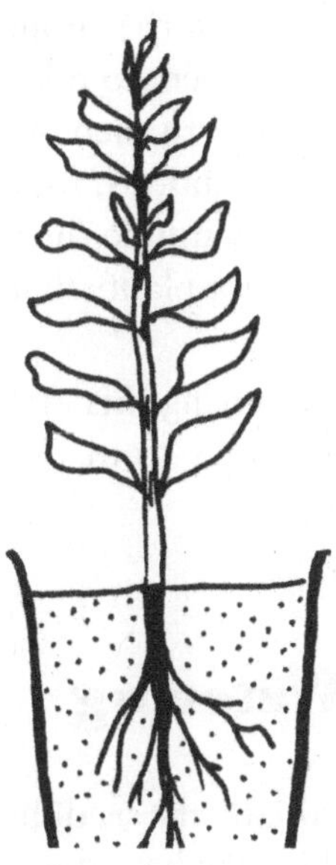

Seedling correctly potted.

The growing-on phase

For the first two weeks, help to overcome the shock of transplanting by keeping the seedlings in a position that provides total shade and protection from wind. Water at least twice daily. A shade house, verandah, greenhouse or a protected place in the garden are all suitable locations.

After two weeks begin the **hardening-off** process.

1. Gradually expose seedlings to morning sunshine, beginning with 30 minutes and increasing slowly until they tolerate a full morning in the sun. At no stage should the sides of the tubes be exposed to direct sun, as this dries out the soil too quickly and causes vapour to form, which may lead to fungal disease. Continue to protect the young plants from wind.
2. When the young trees can handle full sun, gradually harden them to tolerate wind. It is a mistake to foster lush, soft growth then expect the young trees to survive under hard conditions, for they will simply die. The idea is to gradually mimic the trees' final location. That way you will produce plants that will be vigorous and long-lived.

During this growing-on phase it is necessary to protect the seedlings from insect attack, as well as keep the soil free of weeds.

Watering

Initially the seedlings need to be watered at least twice daily, but this may be reduced to once daily after two weeks, depending on the climate.

You may use an overhead watering method with a fine spray, or water from the bottom up by standing the containers in a tray of water until the surface of the soil is moist.

Remember that watering from the bottom up is recommended to safeguard against fungal disease, as this reduces moisture around the stem and leaves. If damping off is a problem in your area, avoid overhead watering late in the day.

Eucalypts in particular should not be overwatered.

During the hardening-off process, gradually reduce watering but don't let the plants wilt. Remember that each plant has only a small amount of soil in which to store moisture, so take care not to drought-stress the seedling.

Fertiliser

It is not wise to overfeed young transplanted trees, as this will cause them to grow too fast and become pot-bound. In addition, soft seedlings, reliant on perfect conditions, do not respond well when planted out into paddock locations where poor soil and harsh weather conditions are the order of the day. However, if your young trees lack colour or are not growing after transplanting, a slow-release fertiliser can be added to the soil mix or a soluble fertiliser applied regularly.

Some people recommend the routine application of a slow-release fertiliser four weeks after pricking out, to ensure steady growth.

Chapter 6

Planting out

The right season

Ideally, seedlings should be planted out when the soil is moist and the ground warm, with no danger of frost – and the day overcast and cool to warm, with no wind.

As Australia is such a vast and varied landscape it is not possible to make exact rules; however, the following points are a guide.

- In dry areas, very late winter is usually a good time.
- In most other areas spring is often the best choice, especially in cold, frosty places and where waterlogging is a problem.
- Autumn after good rain (April, May or even early June) is suitable in areas not affected by frosts, flooding, waterlogging or severe cold. Plant while the soil is still slightly warm, but moist from recent rains.
- Winter is not a good time, especially if soils are heavy, cold and badly drained.
- Late spring and early summer plantings are risky unless you get summer rain or are prepared to water throughout the summer. However in some

areas, species such as *Eucalyptus citriodora* (lemon-scented gum) respond very favourably to planting at this time of the year, even with minimal moisture.

The plant: when is it ready?

Younger seedling trees or shrubs (8–12 months old) will usually outgrow older, more leafy plants that have been repotted. Ideally, the seedling should be about twice the height of the tube or container; however, a vigorous plant the same height as the root depth will give very good results.

The seedling should be sturdy with firm green foliage: a well hardened-off plant ready for life in the big outside world. The stem should be straight with well-formed branches, supported by a strong root system. There should be many thin secondary roots forming a network to the full extent of the soil, so that when the plant is removed from the tube or container soil doesn't fall away; nor should the plant be pot-bound, with tangled, knotted roots. Dense white root tips should be just visible, roots eager to push out into real earth.

Soil preparation

Most Australian trees and shrubs prefer well-drained sandy soil or loam that is acid; however, some have adapted to grow well in poorly drained areas and others in clay.

The drainage and texture of clay soils can be improved by adding gypsum, humus and coarse river sand. On the other hand, species such as the boronias need to be kept moist, so for light soil the addition of peat is recommended to help retain moisture.

Regardless of soil type, the soil should be prepared to create a moist friable bed for your plants, and grass and weed competition should be removed.

Preparation for **larger planting projects** usually follows these two steps.

1. Ripping to loosen and aerate the soil and encourage deep, rapid root growth.
2. Discing or rotary hoeing to turn over grasses and weeds and to break up and level large clods of earth.

For **smaller projects**, weeds may be chipped away or pulled out by hand at each planting site before digging.

Preparation and transport of containers

1. Soak containers and tubes overnight in tubs of water before planting the following day.
2. Remove any weeds and prune off leaves or twigs damaged or weakened in any way.
3. On the following morning, pack tubes and containers tightly in cardboard or polystyrene boxes to avoid damage to stems and foliage.
4. Collect spades and buckets.
5. Plant as soon as possible. Do not leave your plants in a hot vehicle.

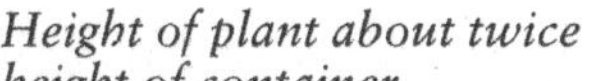

Height of plant about twice height of container.

Sturdy plant, 'hardened off' by exposure to true outdoor environment.

No damage–fungal, mechanical or from insects.

Foliage: healthy, actively growing, even colouring; true to type for species.

Straight stem; well-formed branches if appropriate.

Easy to read, waterproof labelling.

Roots: straight, dense, white, well-developed; not too many protruding from container.

Container: weed-free; deep to ensure long root systems.

How to plant out

1. Select the position for the plant.
2. Remove any weeds or grass from the immediate area.
3. Dig the hole, using a spade. Dig it twice as large as the tube or container and crumble all the loose soil. Put aside any stones; these can be used later to hold down mulch. If the hole fills with water, delay planting until the soil is less waterlogged. If the soil is dry, add water and allow it to soak in.
4. Take the plant from its tube or container.

   To remove a plant from a **tube**, undo the tie and unroll the tube carefully so that the core of soil (and roots) is undisturbed. Old scissors or secateurs may be used to cut open stubborn tubes.

   To remove a plant from a **container**, place your hand over the top of the pot with the stem held loosely between your middle fingers. Turn the pot upside down and tap the bottom of the container against something solid, for example a fence post. Now gently squeeze, shake and tap the pot and ease the plant carefully from the container. If it is well watered it should come away easily, without disturbing the roots.
5. Check the roots. If they are tightly interwoven and matted, loosen and tease them out a little. If some roots are curled, trim off the kinks with your fingers so that they will grow straight when planted.
6. Place the plant in the hole, in line with the natural soil level. If the plant is positioned too low its stem may rot as a result of waterlogging. If it is planted too high its roots will dry out and be overheated; in addition, the surface roots are likely to become exposed as a result

of the action of wind and rain. In sandy conditions it is a good idea to position the plant slightly below ground level, so that during rain the water will run towards the plant rather than away from it.

7. Support the plant with one hand while you use the other to fill the hole with crumbled soil. Gently but firmly pack the loose soil around the plant. Then firm the soil, using the balls of your feet.
8. Water the plant in, to close off any air pockets and settle the soil around the roots. With your bucket held at ground level, slowly and carefully tip water around the plant.
9. Spread mulch around the plant. For details see pages 96–98.
10. Erect a tree guard. For details see pages 99–100.

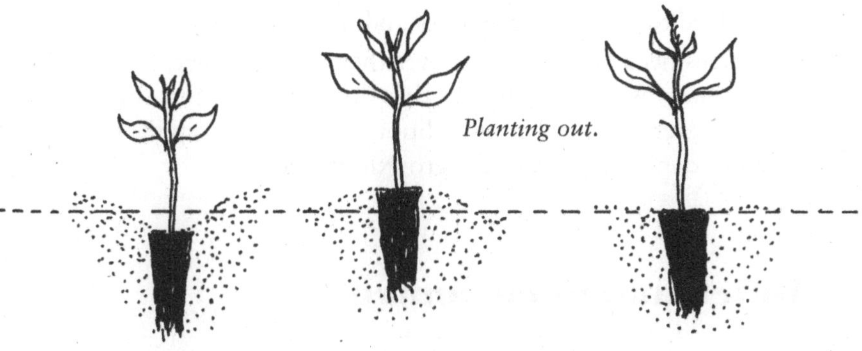

Planting out.

Watering

After planting out, all young trees and shrubs need to be watered in very well. However, if seasonal conditions are favourable and the plant is suited to the locality, this may be the last time the plant needs to be artificially watered. Here are some additional hints.

- A thorough watering once a week encourages plants to grow deep, strong root systems that are more likely to be drought resistant.
- Let the soil dry out between waterings, as this will allow the soil to aerate properly.
- More frequent shallow watering leads to the development of surface roots that dry out. As a result, the plant may die quite suddenly during an unexpected hot spell of weather.
- Overwatering may cause death, as a result of waterlogged soil.
- The boronias, the mint bushes, some callistemons and tea-trees and many other small shrubs need to be watered throughout a dry summer spell, as these species have evolved to grow beside creeks and in boggy areas.
- If trees need to be watered over their first summer, there are many water-bag devices that drip-feed water to young trees over 3–4 weeks. In addition, these bags keep the roots cool and prevent the growth of weeds.

Mulch and weed control

A layer of protective material spread around the newly planted seedling will function as follows.

- Reduce weed and grass growth.
- Keep the roots protected from high temperatures, especially in mid-summer.
- Conserve moisture by preventing the surface soil from drying out too quickly.
- Prevent crusting and erosion of newly disturbed soil.

Your choice of mulch will depend on such factors as cost, availability, labour, soil type and species to be planted, so no single mulch can claim to be ideal for all conditions. A combination is usually the most effective, for example 4–5 sheets of newspaper beneath a layer of seaweed, or pine needles beneath river pebbles. Here are some of the options.

- River stones and pebbles, coarse sand or gravel, crushed rock.
- Wood shavings, wood chips, pine bark, sawdust, shredded poplar wood.
- Pine needles, she-oak needles.
- Leaf mould, bush litter, shredded twigs and leaves.
- Well-aged lawn clippings, well-rotted compost.
- Seaweed, straw (hay contains too many grass and weed seeds to be recommended as a mulching material).
- Shredded paper, newspaper, cardboard.
- Sheet plastic, woven plastic.
- Old carpet, underlay, hessian bags.
- Mulch mats made from recycled paper and cardboard. These rigid square paper-pulp mats are cheap, last at least one year, are biodegradable and contain no plastics or chemicals.
- Ezy-wool mulch, a light felt-like product made from coarse, coloured wool. Easy to spread, environment-friendly, very effective and looks good – but it does cost more than loose mulches.

Spread bulk mulch evenly to a depth of 7–15 cm, and keep mulch free of the trunk of the seedling tree. Collar rot (a fungal disease that can be fatal) may occur if mulch is piled up around the stem.

Wood and bark-based mulches tend to take nitrogen from the soil as they decompose. This is not a problem with acacias or allocasuarinas and casuarinas, as these genera fix their own nitrogen, nor is it a difficulty in very fertile soils. However, if the soils are poor and for other genera, it is advisable to add a little nitrogen fertiliser to bark or wood-based mulches.

Black plastic absorbs heat and increases soil temperature. In a similar way, a dark-coloured mulch absorbs more heat and so reduces the risk of frost damage, whereas a light-coloured mulch can actually increase frost damage. So select the colour of your mulch carefully in frost-prone and hot areas.

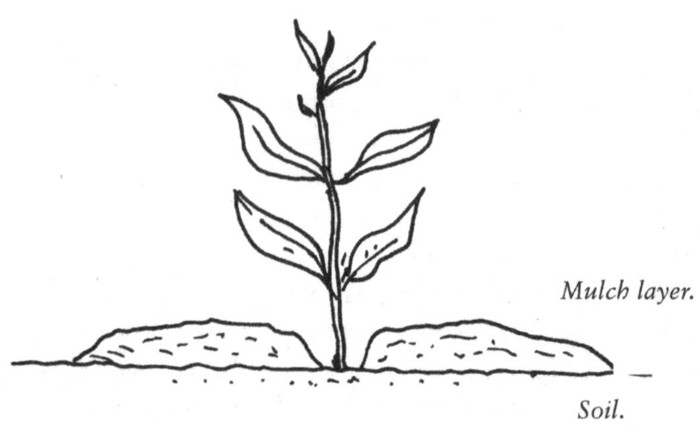

Mulching.

Note: Not placed against stem.

Tree guards and stakes

There are many different types of guard you can use to protect trees from wind, sun, frost, rabbits and hares, wallabies and kangaroos, sheep and cattle, mowers, pets and children.

Sometimes a temporary or permanent fence is cheaper and easier to erect than individual tree guards; however, regardless of the type of protection you choose, it must be effective immediately after planting – the next day is often too late! The following are some options.

- White shadecloth, woven plastic sheet, flexible plastic mesh, hessian bags, second-hand plastic bags (fertiliser or feed bags, shopping bags) – all with 3 stakes. Hessian is a particularly good material to use when protecting plants against sun, as it provides shade as well as good air circulation. In frost-prone areas, plastic, hessian and cardboard are useful materials.
- Rigid plastic mesh with 2 stakes or 3 pegs.
- Plastic tubes with 3–4 stakes.
- Car tyres (these usually protect young trees from rabbits and hares).
- Chicken wire or rabbit netting with 2–3 stakes or pegs.
- Heavy gauge mesh with 3 steel posts (these are useful to protect young trees from cattle).
- Bottle-top blanks with 2–3 stakes for a single sheet, or 3 pegs for a more rigid double sheet. This product is the tin-plate mesh that remains after bottle-tops are cut out. Handle carefully, as it has very sharp edges. Eventually it rusts away, but it is very cheap and effective, and certainly lasts long enough to protect the tree in that critical early stage of development.
- Milk cartons, with 2 stakes or pegs.

- Tree guards with wire that has an electric current running through it. Excellent for goats!

Where wind is a problem, any mesh-type material is helpful in reducing wind damage to the root structure and branches of the young tree and shrub.

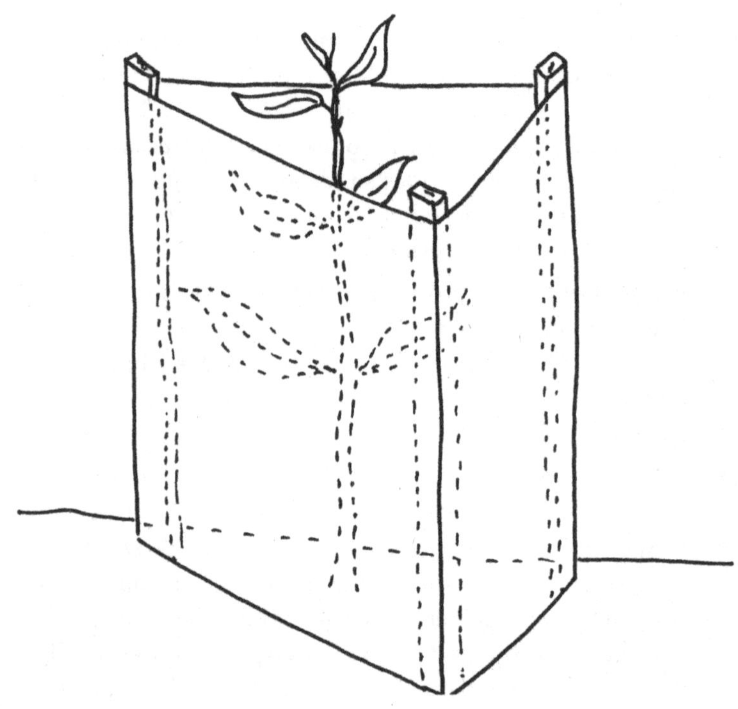

Wind guards aid in first season tree survival.

Stakes for support

The most popular stakes for support of trees and guards are hardwood, steel and bamboo. Hardwood and steel are long-lasting and suitable for use in stony ground, whereas bamboo is light-weight and useful in soft soil only.

If a tree guard is not necessary, but very strong wind is a consideration, two or three stakes may be used to support the tree in its early stage of growth.

Ideally, these stakes should be driven in before planting the tree, to avoid root damage. Using a figure-of-eight loop, tie any elastic material (old ties or pantyhose are suitable) around the tree and between the stakes. It is necessary to check the tie regularly for any sign of chafing or ringbarking on the trunk.

The tie needs to be loose so that the roots and trunk move enough to develop strength, but with sufficient support to protect the roots from becoming so loose and weak they cause the tree to die. Success depends on a balance between too much and not enough support in this critical period of early growth.

In very windy conditions, soft fencing wire threaded through old garden hose is ideal for steadying young tree trunks.

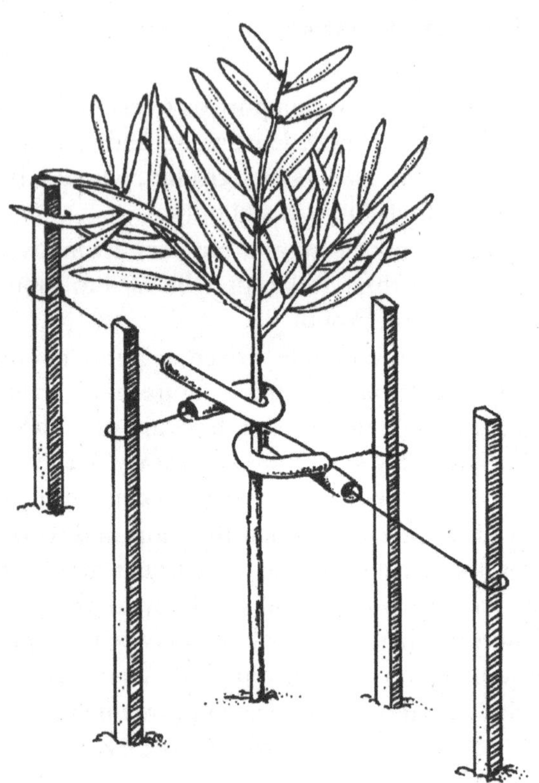

Pests

Grubs, caterpillars, insects, spiders and many other creatures make up the complex web of life that surrounds us. All are important parts of the natural food chain and as such should never be sprayed with pesticides.

Small infestations will be controlled by birds, frogs and lizards and will do little damage. Their nibbling often has no more impact than a light pruning.

If there is a severe outbreak of one pest in particular, use organic pest-control measures such as barriers, traps and sprays

(using products like bicarbonate of soda, milk, flour, pure soap and herbs).

If caterpillars are stripping your young plants, pick them off by hand and squash them beneath your shoe. Remember, it is neither necessary nor advisable to kill every single caterpillar off every plant. Your aim should be to simply tip the balance in favour of the plant!

Fertiliser

Many of our Australian plants have evolved to grow in very poor soils. For this reason, the question of fertiliser needs to be handled with care, for overfeeding leads to plants producing an overabundance of softwood and leafy growth, rather than sturdier branches with plentiful flowers. Too much fertiliser can also shorten life, as the foliage and root systems are frequently out of balance.

Grevilleas, banksias, dryandras, hakeas and acacias are very sensitive to the high levels of phosphorus that occur in some fertilisers, for their evolution has taken place on leached heathland soils and sandy plains. On the other hand, plants that grow in the rainforests of New South Wales and Queensland are able to tolerate high levels of phosphorus.

Acacias, allocasuarinas and casuarinas do not need any fertiliser as they have the ability to fix nitrogen in the soil by means of their root nodules. These three genera enrich the soil for other more delicate plants.

Animal manures, even after lengthy ageing, may be harmful to Australian native plants, so save these for your vegetable garden.

If fertiliser is required, use either of the following, but keep their use to a minimum.

- Blood and bone powder can be used to stimulate sluggish plants. The odour repels rabbits; but it attracts dogs, foxes and cats, and this may be a problem. Work it in well and water thoroughly.
- Slow-release pellets are convenient and easy to use.

Fertiliser may be applied during the soil-preparation stage or used in the actual planting-out process. With established plants, apply fertiliser beyond the canopy, in holes made with a fork. This will encourage the roots to grow outwards and give the plant greater stability. Apply in late winter or early spring, but keep levels low.

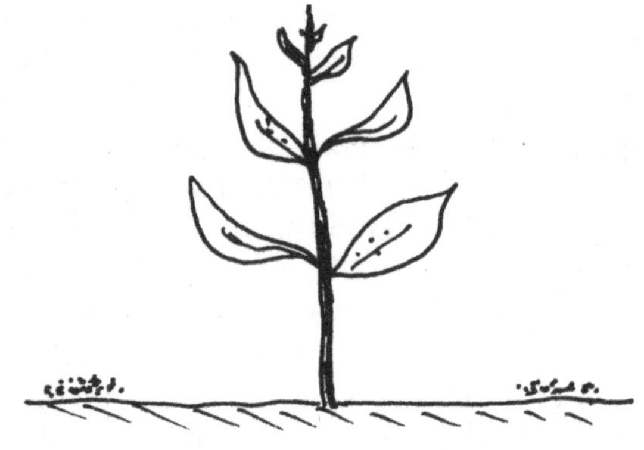

15 cm.

Fertilising young trees.

(Circular band – 15 cm from trunk.)

Pruning

Most Australian native plants benefit from light pruning. The aim is to promote bushy growth and so reduce straggly branches that whip about in windy conditions. Life span is usually increased by pruning, especially with quick-growing trees and shrubs.

Pruning is normally left until after flowering and is commenced when the plant is relatively young. Use the following hints to help you.

- Prune regularly and lightly rather than cutting back occasionally and severely.
- Do not prune in very hot or frosty weather.
- Use clean, sharp secateurs and so avoid injuring the plant and introducing disease.
- Prune away all dead wood.
- Water well after pruning.

There are two recommended methods.

- **Method 1.** Pinch out soft tips during the growing period, to stimulate bushy growth. Use secateurs or your finger and thumb.
- **Method 2.** Prune back to a shoot or a branch with leaves, with the cut just above the shoot or leafy branch. Cuts should be sloped to ensure that moisture drains away from the plant and doesn't settle in pockets. Cut no further back than two-year-old wood – preferably concentrate on part of the previous year's growth.

Acacias may be pruned after flowering, but not too hard: never cut back to leafless wood. Pruning will prevent them becoming straggly and woody, as well as prolonging their life.

Boobiallas can be trimmed to form an attractive thick hedge.

Boronias, croweas and many other small shrubs benefit from regular tip pruning. This encourages dense, compact growth and abundant flowers.

Callistemons, calothamnus, grevilleas and banksias may have their blooms cut each year for floral display. This practice will promote bushy growth as well as ensuring plentiful flowers for the following years.

Eucalypts of the multi-stemmed mallee type can be cut right back to ground level to promote attractive new growth.

Chapter 7

Botanical and common names made easy

The way we name humans and plants is very similar.

Classification	*Human*	*Plant*
Race / plant family	Irish	Proteaceae
Surname / plant genus (pl. genera)	O'Brady	*Banksia*
Given name / plant species	Patrick	*serrata*
Nickname/ plant common name	Ginger (Pat has red hair)	Saw banksia (leaves have serrated edge)

Patrick O'Brady (Ginger) is of Irish blood, and *Banksia serrata* (saw banksia) is from the Proteaceae family of plants.

Once you understand how **botanical names** are put together in Latin form you will find their study rewarding, as they may describe plant characteristics that **common names** may not refer to.

Plants can be named after a person, for example the banksia was named after Sir Joseph Banks, the British botanist who travelled to Australia in 1770 with Captain

Cook, and the grevillea after C. F. Greville, a patron of botany. Sometimes the second word in the botanical name is made from the name of the person who discovered the plant. Or a plant can have a name that comes from Latin or Greek words put together to describe certain characteristics; two examples follow.

- 'Leptospermum' comes from two Greek words: *leptos*, slender and fine, and *sperma*, spore or seed. All plants in this group have fine seed.
- 'Callistemon' comes the Greek *kalos*, beautiful, and *stemon*, which became the Latin word *stamen*. All plants in this group have beautiful stamens, making up the well-known bottlebrush flower.

Here are two more examples of how plant names are made up.

- *Callistemon citrinus*. We already know that this plant will have bottlebrush flowers. The second part of the name comes from the Latin word *citrus*, citron tree; plants with *citrinus* as part of their name will have lemon-scented foliage.
- *Eucalyptus citriodora*. The first part of the name is made up of two Greek words: *eu*, well, and *kaluptos*, covered. All plants in this group will have a cap covering each flower bud. The second part of the name, *citriodora*, traces back to the Latin word *citrus*. This plant also has lemon-scented leaves.

Are you beginning to see a pattern now, a meaning behind the naming system? Well, before you become too confident, a word of warning! If plants share the same genus name ('surname') they are indeed closely related and have many common characteristics, especially in their flowers; for example *Grevillea*

robusta and *Grevillea alpina* share spidery flowers and have thin-walled seed pods. However, having the same species name ('given name') means nothing at all; for example, *Acacia pulchella* and *Banksia pulchella* are not related in any way.

Another trap for beginners can be a name such as *Grevillea banksii.* This spectacular plant, producing large groups of beautiful scarlet flowers at the ends of branches, is a grevillea, not a banksia. It was named after Sir Joseph Banks because of its dramatic flowers, not because it shares any common features with the banksia genus.

So it is the genus name (the first word in the botanical name) that supplies the most important facts, with the species name (the second word) simply adding a little extra information.

Common names for plants are like nicknames and often seem easier to remember than botanical names; however, they can be confusing, as they often differ from place to place and there is often more than one common name for the same plant. For example the name 'black wattle' is used for at least two species of acacia, as well as a plant from another genus. And prickly Moses is a different plant in Victoria, New South Wales and Western Australia!

The following is a list of common names given to various genera.

Genus	***Common name***
Acacia	Wattle
Angophora	Apple box
Anigozanthos	Kangaroo paw
Banksia	Honeysuckle
Callistemon	Bottlebrush
Carpobrotus	Pigface
Allocasuarina, Casuarina	She-oak, buloke

Genus	*Common name*
Calothamnus	Net-bush, one-sided bottlebrush
Chamelaucium	Wax flower
Clematis	Traveller's joy, white beard
Crinum	Lily
Dillwynia	Eggs and bacon
Epacris	Heath
Eriostemon	Wax flower
Eucalyptus	Gum tree
Grevillea	Spider flower
Hakea	Needle-bush
Hardenbergia	False sarsaparilla, coral-pea
Helichrysum	Everlasting daisy
Kennedia	Red bean, coral vine, running postman
Leptospermum	Tea-tree
Melaleuca	Paperback, honey-myrtle
Myoporum	Boobialla
Nuytsia	Western Australian Christmas tree
Olearia	Daisy bush
Patersonia	Native iris
Prostanthera	Mint bush
Telopea	Waratah
Tetratheca	Black-eyed Susan
Woollsia	Heath
Xanthorrhoea	Black boy, grass tree

For some plants the genus name is used like a common name and the plant has no other common name; for example boronia, correa, dryandra and thryptomene. On the other hand, when a common name has replaced both the genus and species name, this common name is often widely known and used.

The following table lists the botanical and common names for a number of native plants.

Botanical name	***Common name***
Acacia acinacea	Gold-dust wattle
A. aculeatissima	Thin-leaf wattle
A. alata	Winged wattle
A. baileyana	Cootamundra wattle
A. brachybotrya	Grey mulga
A. brownii	Dwarf prickly Moses
A. buxifolia	Box-leaf wattle
A. cardiophylla	Wyalong wattle
A. colletioides	Wait-a-while wattle
A. continua	Thorn wattle
A. dealbata	Silver wattle
A. decora	Showy wattle
A. elongata	Swamp wattle
A. genistifolia	Spreading wattle
A. gladiiformis	Sword-leaf wattle
A. hakeoides	Hakea-leaf wattle
A. howittii	Sticky wattle
A. iteaphylla	Willow-leafed wattle
A. longifolia	Sallow, Sydney golden wattle
A. mearnsii	Black wattle
A. melanoxylon	Blackwood
A. neriifolia	Silver wattle

Botanical name	*Common name*
A. paradoxa	Kangaroo thorn, hedge wattle
A. pravissima	Ovens wattle
A. pulchella	Western prickly Moses
A. pycnantha	Golden wattle
A. retinodes	Wirilda wattle
A. rubida	Red-stemmed wattle
A. rupicola	Rock wattle
A. siculiformis	Dagger wattle
A. spinescens	Spiny wattle
A. stricta	Hop wattle
A. suaveolens	Sweet-scented wattle
A. terminalis	Cedar wattle
A. ulicifolia	Prickly Moses
A. vernicflua	Varnish wattle
Acmena (syn. *Eugenia*) *smithii*	Lilly-pilly
Agonis flexuosa	Willow myrtle
Albizja distachya	Cape wattle
A. lophantha	Cape Leeuwin wattle
Allocasuarina verticillata	Drooping she-oak
Alyogyne huegelii	Lilac hibiscus
Angophora cordifolia	Dwarf apple
Anigozanthos flavidus	Yellow kangaroo paw
A. manglesii	Red-stemmed green kangaroo paw
A. viridis	Green kangaroo paw
Banksia coccinea	Scarlet banksia
B. ericifolia	Heath banksia
B. grandis	Bull banksia
B. integrifolia	Coast banksia

Botanical name	*Common name*
B. marginata	Silver banksia
B. media	Golden stalk banksia
B. ornata	Desert banksia
B. prionotes	Acorn banksia
B. pulchella	Teasel banksia
B. quercifolia	Oak-leafed banksia
B. serrata	Saw banksia
B. speciosa	Showy banksia
B. spinulosa	Hill or hairpin banksia
Boronia megastigma	Brown or scented boronia
Callistemon brachyandrus	Prickly bottlebrush
C. citrinus	Crimson bottlebrush
C. linearis	Narrow-leaf bottlebrush
C. pinifolius	Green-flowering bottlebrush
C. salignus	Willow bottlebrush
C. speciosus	Common bottlebrush
C. viminalis	Weeping bottlebrush
C. violaceus	Violet bottlebrush
Calothamnus gilesii	Giles net-bush
C. quadrifidus	Crimson cluster net-bush
C. sanguineus	Blood-red net-bush
C. villosus	Woolly net-bush
Cassia artemisiodes	Silver cassia
Casuarina cunninghamiana	River she-oak
C. glauca	Swamp oak
Ceratopetalum gummiferum	NSW Christmas bush
Chamelaucium uncinatum	Geraldton wax flower
Clematis aristata	Traveller's joy, white beard
Clianthus formosus	Sturt desert pea

Botanical name	*Common name*
Correa alba	White correa
C. reflexa	Common correa
Dryandra formosa	Showy dryandra
Epacris impressa	Common heath
Eucalyptus albens	White box
E. alpina	Grampians gum
E. caesia	Gungurru
E. camaldulensis	River red gum
E. cinerea	Argyle apple, mealy stringybark
E. citriodora	Lemon-scented gum
E. cladocalyx	Sugar gum
E. dives	Broad-leaved peppermint
E. ficifolia	Red flowering gum
E. globulus	Tasmanian blue gum
E. lehmannii	Bushy yate
E. leucoxylon rosea	Yellow gum, pink-flowered
E. macrorhyncha	Red stringybark
E. maculata	Spotted gum
E. melliodora	Yellow box
E. microcarpa	Grey box
E. nicholii	Narrow-leafed peppermint
E. obliqua	Messmate
E. ovata	Swamp gum
E. pauciflora	Snow gum
E. polyanthemos	Red box
E. rubida	Candlebark
E. saligna	Sydney blue gum
E. sideroxylon	Red ironbark
E. spathulata	Swamp mallet

Botanical name	*Common name*
E. viminalis	Manna gum
E. viridis	Green mallee
Grevillea aquifolium	Prickly or Grampians grevillea
G. banksii	Banks' grevillea
G. hookeriana	Toothbrush grevillea
G. longifolia	Fern-leaf grevillea
G. robusta	Silky oak
G. rosmarinifolia	Rosemary grevillea
Hakea erinacea	Hedgehog hakea
H. laurina	Pincushion hakea
H. petiolaris	Sea urchin hakea
H. sericea	Silky hakea
H. suaveolens	Sweet-scented hakea
H. victoriae	Royal hakea
Hardenbergia comptoniana	Blue coral-pea, native wistaria
H. violacea	False sarsaparilla, purple coral-pea
Helichrysum apiculatum	Common everlasting
H. bracteatum	Golden everlasting
Hibiscus splendens	Hibiscus
Kennedia coccinea	Coral vine
K. prostrata	Running postman
K. rubicunda	Dusky coral-pea
Leptospermum laevigatum	Coast tea-tree
L. rotundifolium	Round-leaf tea-tree
Melaleuca armillaris	Bracelet honey-myrtle
M. decussata	Gross-leaf honey-myrtle
M. ericifolia	Swamp paperbark
M. hypericifolia	Red honey-myrtle

Botanical name	**Common name**
M. incana	Grey honey-myrtle
M. lanceolata	Moonah
M. lateritia	Robin redbreast
M. pulchella	Claw flower
M. squarrosa	Scented paperbark
M. wilsonii	Crimson honey-myrtle
Myoporum insulare	Boobialla
Pittosporum undulatum	Sweet pittosporum
Telopea speciosissima	NSW waratah
Thryptomene calycina	Grampians thryptomene
Xanthorrhoea australis	Black boy or grass tree
Xylomelum pyriforme	Woody pear

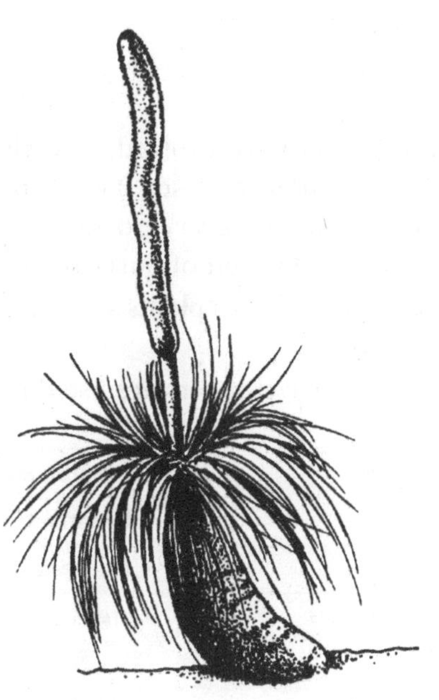

*Black boy or grass tree (*Xanthorrhoea *species).*

Chapter 8

Trees and shrubs for special situations

Australian plants have evolved to withstand amazing extremes of climate and soil type. In addition, they have developed to suit every possible circumstance, for example the revegetation of burnt or eroded areas.

This chapter includes plants suitable for a number of specific situations.

Some attractive climbers are listed below.

Botanical name	***Common name***
Clematis	Clematis, traveller's joy
Hardenbergia	Coral-pea, false sarsaparilla
Hibbertia scandens	Large twining guinea-flower
Hoya australis	Wax flower
Kennedia	Coral vine, running postman
Marianthus	Orange bell climber
Pandorea pandorana	Wonga vine
Passiflora cinnabarina	Red passionflower

These plants are able to tolerate salt spray and saline conditions in general.

Botanical name	***Common name***
Acacia floribunda	Catkin wattle
A. longifolia	Sallow, Sydney golden wattle
A. pycnantha	Golden wattle
A. sophorae	Coast wattle
Allocasuarina verticillata	Drooping she-oak
Alyxia buxiflora	Sea box
Atriplex	Saltbushes
Banksia integrifolia	Coast banksia
B. marginata	Silver banksia
B. serrata	Saw banksia
Callistemon citrinus	Crimson bottlebrush
Calocephalus brownii	Cushion bush
Calothamnus quadrifidus	Crimson cluster net-bush
C. villosus	Woolly net-bush
Casuarina cunninghamiana	River she-oak
C. glauca	Swamp oak
Correa alba	White correa
Dryandra formosa	Showy dryandra
Eucalyptus camaldulensis	Red gum
E. cornuta	Yate
E. leucoxylon	Yellow gum
E. occidentalis	Swamp yate
E. sargentii	Sargent's mallet
E. viminalis	Manna gum
Hakea suaveolens	Sweet-scented hakea
Kunzea ambigua	White kunzea

Botanical name	*Common name*
K. baxteri	Baxter's kunzea
Leptospermum laevigatum	Coast tea-tree
Melaleuca armillaris	Bracelet honey-myrtle
M. decussata	Cross-leaf honey-myrtle
M. ericifolia	Swamp paperbark
M. halmaturorum	Kangaroo paperbark
M. hypericifolia	Red honey-myrtle
M. lanceolata	Moonah
M. nesophila	Lavender paperbark
Myoporum insulare	Boobialla
Rhagodia nutans	Nodding saltbush
Westringia fruticosa	Austral rosemary

Red box.

The following trees are able to grow well in cold wet climates.

Botanical name	***Common name***
Acacia longifolia	Sallow, Sydney golden wattle
A. melanoxylon	Blackwood
Casuarina cunninghamiana	River she-oak
C. glauca	Swamp oak
Eucalyptus botryoides	Southern mahogany
E. camaldulensis	Red gum
E. kitsoniana	Bog gum
E. largiflorens	Black box
E. occidentalis	Swamp yate
E. ovata	Swamp gum
E. robusta	Swamp mahogany
E. sargentii	Sargent's mallet
E. spathulata	Swamp mallet
E. viminalis	Manna gum
Melaleuca ericifolia	Swamp paperbark
M. halmaturorum	Kangaroo paperbark
M. lanceolata	Moonah
M. squarrosa	Scented paperbark
M. styphelioides	Prickly-leaf paperbark

Trees that bind the soil and help stabilise eroded areas include the following.

Botanical name	***Common name***
Acacia longfolia	Sallow, Sydney golden wattle
A. melanoxylon	Blackwood
A. saligna	Golden wreath wattle
Casuarina cunniughamiana	River she-oak
Eucalyptus camaldulensis	Red gum
E. microcarpa	Grey box
Melaleuca	Paperbarks, honey-myrtles

White ironbark.

The following plants are able to grow in hot, dry areas.

Botanical name	***Common name***
Acacia calamifolia	Wallowa
A. farnesiana	Sponge wattle
A. pendula	Weeping myall
Calothamnus sanguineus	Blood-red net-bush
C. villosus	Woolly net-bush
Callitris verrucosa	Mallee cypress-pine
Cassia eremophila	Desert cassia
Conospermum triplinervium	Tree smoke-bush
Eucalyptus angulosa	Ridge-fruited mallee
E. forrestiana	Forrest's marlock
E. tetraptera	Four-winged mallee gum
E. torquata	Coral gum
Hakea multilineata	Grass-leaf hakea
H. purpurea	Purple-flowered hakea
Hibiscus heterophyllus	Native rosella

Hot, moist conditions are suitable for the following plants.

Botanical name	***Common name***
Acacia subporosa	River wattle
Anigozanthos viridis	Green kangaroo paw
Banksia coccinea	Scarlet banksia
B. ericifolia	Heath banksia
Beaufortia sparsa	Gravel bottlebrush
Callistemon	Bottlebrushes
Calytrix fraseri	Summer fringe-myrtle
Ceratopetalum gummiferum	NSW Christmas bush
Grevillea robusta	Silky oak
Kunzea	Kunzeas
Leptospermum	Tea-trees
Melaleuca	Honey-myrtles and paperbarks
Patersonia	Native iris

For rapid growth, acacias are a good choice. However, fast growers usually have a short life, so establish longer-lived trees in the shelter of the faster-growing plants. Careful pruning will prolong the life of the quick-growing plants listed below.

Botanical name	***Common name***
Acacia longifolia	Sallow, Sydney golden wattle
A. saligna	Golden wreath wattle
A. sophorae	Coast wattle
Albizia distachya	Cape wattle
Eucalyptus	Gums, mallees, boxes
Grevillea aquifolium	Prickly or Grampians grevillea
C. longifolia	Fern-leaf grevillea
Hakea laurina	Pincushion hakea
H. multilineata	Grass-leaf hakea
Kunzea baxteri	Baxter's kunzea
K. peduncularis	Burgan
Melaleuca ericifolia	Swamp paperbark
M. squarrosa	Scented paperbark
Myoporum	Boobiallas

There are many trees and shrubs that provide good wind protection. Here are a few to try.

Botanical name	***Common name***
Acacia buxifolia	Box-leaf wattle
A. howittii	Sticky wattle
Acmena (syn. Eugenia) smithii	Lilly-pilly
Alyxia buxifolia	Sea-box
Banksia serrata	Saw banksia
Callistemon citrinus	Crimson bottlebrush
C. phoeniceus	Lesser bottlebrush
Callitris verrucosa	Mallee cypress-pine
Eucalyptus cladocalyx	Sugar gum (dwarf type)
E. leucoxylon	Yellow gum
Grevillea rosmarinifolia	Rosemary grevillea
Hakea elliptica	Oval-leaf hakea
H. suaveolens	Sweet-scented hakea
Leptospermum laevigatum	Coast tea-tree
Melaleuca hypericifolia	Red honey-myrtle
M. squarrosa	Scented paperbark
Myoporum insulare	Boobialla
Syzygium australe	Brush cherry

Identification by flower and seed

Chapter 9

The tables in this chapter will enable you to accurately classify many Australian plants. However, it is sometimes necessary to seek the advice of an expert for positive identification.

Some plant families, their flowers and seed

Family	*Genus*	*Flower*	*Seed*
Myrtaceae	*Eucalyptus* *Melaleuca* *Callistemon* *Leptospermum* *Calothamnus*	Five petals or bundles of stamens attached to receptacle.	Held in woody capsule below base of flower.
Proteaceae	*Banksia* *Hakea* *Grevillea*	Curved, spider-like flowers, often clustered in large spikes or heads.	Held in hard woody cone or nut, or thin-walled pod.
Mimosaceae	*Acacia* *Albizia*	Clusters of yellow stamens in balls or spikes.	Held in typical legume pod. Seed has stalk connecting it to pod.
Papilionaceae	*Kennedia* *Hardenbergia*	Pea-shaped flowers on climbing or trailing plant.	Held in typical legume pod.

How to identify genus within the family Myrtaceae

Genus	*Flower*	*Seed capsule*
Leptospermum (tea-tree) Over 80 species of shrubs and small trees.	Open, with five petals and many stamens.	Small woody capsule containing many narrow seeds. The thinner-walled capsules drop seed annually. The more woody ones enclose seed indefinitely, waiting for bushfire.
Calothamnus (net-bush, or one-sided bottlebrush) Over 26 species of medium-size bushes.	Usually arranged on one side of the branch with stamens in bundles.	Small woody capsules containing many narrow seeds.
Melaleuca (paperbark or honey myrtle) Over 200 species of shrubs and trees.	Bottlebrush-type flowers, with stamens grouped in bundles.	Small woody capsules containing many small seeds. Arranged all around branch.
Callistemon (bottlebrush) Over 20 species of shrubs and small trees.	Bottlebrush-type flowers with stamens evenly spaced.	Small woody capsules containing many small seeds. Arranged all around branch.

Eucalyptus (gum, mallee, box, etc.) Over 500 species of small and large trees.	A mass of stamens held together in cup-like receptacle. Small cap covering stamens in bud stage is pushed off as fower bud opens.	Woody gumnut-type fruit: a capsule divided into compartments each containing 'chaff' and tiny seeds. Fruit has distinct rim, showing scar of fallen bud-cap. Seed is released annually, or when branch dies or tree is affected by fire.
Angophora (apple box) 7 species of tree, very closely related to eucalypts.	Adult leaves mostly in opposite pairs along branch, whereas eucalypt leaves are more commonly alternate. Eucalypt-type blossom.	Small woody fruit with no fused cap on seed capsule.

How to identify genus within the family Proteaceae

Genus	*Flower*	*Seed capsule*
Banksia (honeysuckle) Over 73 species of shrubs and small trees.	Mostly slender flowers massed with dense spikes. Vary from small balls to giant candle-shaped.	Thick woody cone scattered with large partly-embedded woody seed capsules. Seeds are released when branch dies or plant is affected by bushfire.
Genus: ***Grevilla*** (spider-flower) Over 250 species of shrubs and trees.	Flowers in clusters or elongated spikes and arranged in tooth-brush, spider, poker or bottle-brush-like groups.	Thin-walled pod containing one or more flat seeds that fall from plant almost immediately.
Hakea (needle-bush) Over 125 species of shrubs and small trees.	Almost identical to those of *Grevillea* except in details of nectar glands at the base of flower.	Distinctive, hard woody fruit, often with pointy beak-like end, that splits in half to release two winged seeds. Each seed fits neatly into grooved depression. Some seeds are retained until bushfire-affected.

Chapter 10

Seed for purpose: an overview

Singly or in groups, the plants you grow from seed can serve a variety of purposes – all of them exciting for the Australian environment.

Landscape design

One seed has the potential to block off an ugly view, reduce noise, help purify the air, and soften glare and dangerous reflections. A single seed can provide protection against wind and rain, as well as give shade and natural beauty to any setting.

There is true power in every seed.

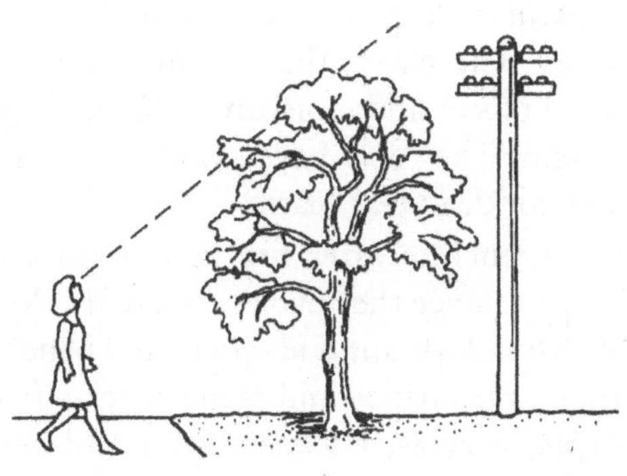

Screening an ugly view.

Fire protection

It is usual to associate trees with the spread of fire; however, *carefully selected* species in well-maintained shelterbelts can actually help prevent bushfire damage to homes, livestock and grassland in the following ways.

- Trees reduce wind speed and therefore the speed and intensity of the fire. Homes and buildings are best protected by a shelterbelt that allows 0–60 per cent of wind to pass through it. This effectively reduces wind speed by 50 per cent.
- Trees catch and deflect burning debris – flaming leaves and twigs that could lodge in roof crevices or beneath verandahs.
- Trees absorb radiant heat and so act as a shield. Dense hedge-like plantings of boobiallas (*Myoporum* species) and sweet pittosporum (*Pittosporum undulatum*), no closer than 6–10 m to buildings, are particularly effective in this regard.
- Trees deflect heat and smoke, important factors in survival of humans and livestock in a bushfire.

Fire-resistant plant species are particularly important in bushfire-prone areas. The plants that are most resistant usually have a high level of salt and moisture in their leaves, along with a low oil content. They also have smooth thick bark and a dense crown without dead leaf matter.

The ability to regenerate after fire is a characteristic of most Australian plants, since they evolved with fire. Many will reshoot: eucalypts from dormant buds protected beneath thick bark; allocasuarinas, casuarinas and some acacias from their roots; and eucalypts, acacias, allocasuarinas and casuarinas from stumps.

Many seeds germinate readily after fire, especially those enclosed in woody capsules, such as banksias, hakeas, tea-trees, callistemons and some eucalypts. Abundant acacia seed lies waiting in the soil for a combination of fire and rain to germinate it. It may wait several decades before bursting into new life.

The following native trees and shrubs are relatively fire-resistant.

Botanical name	*Common name*
Acacia baileyana	Cootamundra wattle
A. cyclops	West Australia coastal wattle
A. glandulicarpa	Hairy pod wattle
A. howittii	Sticky wattle
A. iteaphylla	Willow-leafed wattle
A. melanoxylon	Blackwood
A. pravissima	Ovens wattle
A. prominens	Golden rain wattle
A. terminalis	Cedar wattle
A. vestita	Hairy wattle
*Acmena (*syn. *Eugenia) smithii*	Lilly-pilly
Agonis juniperina	Juniper myrtle
Atigophora costata	Apple jack
Atriplex	Saltbushes
Brachychiton populneus	Kurrajong
Casuarina cristata	Belah
C. cunninghamiana	River she-oak
Eucalyptus maculata	Spotted gum
Ficus macrophylla	Moreton Bay fig
Grevillea rosmarinifolia	Rosemary grevillea
Hakea laurina	Pincushion hakea
H. salicifolia	Willow hakea
H. suaveolens	Sweet hakea
Lagunaria patersonii	Pyramid tree
Melaleuca ericifolia	Swamp paperbark
M. halmaturorum	Kangaroo Island paperbark

Botanical name	*Common name*
M. lanceolata	Moonah
Melia azedarach	White cedar
Myoporum insulare	Boobialla
Pittosporum undulatum	Sweet pittosporum
Tristania conferta	Brush box

Gardens

A large number of Australians are now choosing to grow native plants in their gardens, and many have discovered the joy of growing their own plants from seed.

A garden that has been landscaped to blend into the natural environment creates a feeling of harmony and provides restful areas for outdoor living. Native trees, shrubs, climbing plants, groundcover and flowers can be planted to give shelter from wind, and shade and privacy for barbecue, sitting and play areas,

Spectacular displays of Sturt desert pea, banksias, dryandras, grevilleas and acacias can be created, with hybrid varieties providing extra interest.

A garden that contains a variety of bottlebrush and tubular-shaped flowers will soon become a haven for native birds, which will in turn eat insect pests. So you can live in tune with the natural world and the seasons, and your garden can be an integral part of the Australian landscape.

Native plants are surprisingly adaptable and the majority will grow in most soil types. However, it is wise to choose the position for each plant carefully, noting the amount of sunshine, shelter and moisture that will best suit that particular shrub or tree.

Most Australian plants enjoy a sunny position but there are those that prefer shade, for example correas, ferns, boronias, sweet pittosporum and some acacias.

Wind kills more plants than is generally realised. Quick-growing shelter trees, and stakes, are important to help prevent damage to newly established root structures.

Avoid the temptation to buy large plants: smaller, younger ones will grow much more quickly and mature into stronger, more vigorous plants. Better still, grow your own plants from seed; then you can plant them out at the very best time!

If your soil type is heavy, plants such as Sturt desert pea may be grown from seed in a pot filled with coarse sand and watered only occasionally. This way you can have the thrill of a truly spectacular desert bloom.

Grevilleas, melaleucas and tea-trees make excellent hedges and windbreaks, as well as attracting birds. Sweet-smelling boronia, eucalypts with stunning pink and white trunks, the waratah and the spectacular Christmas bush all offer something different, something Australian.

A well-planned bush garden saves both time and money, as there is less need for digging, watering, weeding and fertiliser. In return for your foresight you will enjoy a relaxing haven where humans, birds, trees and flowers blend to create a feeling of tranquillity.

Reclamation of mining land

Rehabilitation of land degraded by mining operations is now accepted company practice in Australia. Consequently, the mining industry is the largest user of native plant seed. Their broad aim is to re-establish vegetation similar to that which existed before the mining disturbance – and also to minimise soil erosion.

Some container-grown seedlings are used, especially those varieties with seed difficult to germinate or collect. However, most seed is sown directly into the soil, as this method is cheaper and more efficient when large areas are to be planted in a short time.

Aerial seeding is relatively common, while hand-seeding is used with very large seed or in very wet areas. Ground-seeding machines are used widely, drilling a balanced seed mix to ensure that each species is suitably represented (see **Direct seeding** in Chapter 4).

Acacias, eucalypts, allocasuarinas, casuarinas and melaleucas are the most widely planted genera Australia-wide, with acacias and eucalypts the most common, in numbers equal to each other.

The acacias most widely planted include *Acacia holosericea*, *A. longifolia* (sallow or Sydney golden wattle) and *A. pulchella* (western prickly Moses). These are especially important as they grow quickly, fix nitrogen in the soil and produce enormous quantities of seed. The eucalypt most commonly planted is *Eucalyptus crebra* (narrow-leafed red ironbark).

It must be noted, however, that where biodiversity is intended, the use of fast-growing (and seeding) species such as acacias and eucalypts needs to be carefully monitored. Monocultures can easily result, with the competition too fierce for less vigorous species.

Melaleuca armillaris (bracelet honey-myrtle) and *Calothamnus quadrifidus* (crimson cluster net-bush) are also widely used to reclaim land degraded by mining operations.

Salinity control

Land degradation is now a serious problem in Australia, with rising watertables (through irrigation or overclearing) leading to lower productivity because of increased salinity levels and waterlogging.

The use of native seeds in tree-planting programs offers our best defence to reverse this downward trend, as trees use large amounts of water, thus lowering saline watertables.

Hilltops, rocky ridges and gullies are critical sites that require immediate attention with the planting of species suited to the soil type and climate of the locality. In irrigation areas *Casuarina obesa* and *Casuarina glauca* (both called swamp oak) are particularly tolerant to salt and waterlogging, and have been used extensively.

Soil erosion

Australian soils are both fragile and ancient in structure and have been severely eroded since white settlement. Too many trees have been cleared from farming land, and a combination of overstocking and severe climatic conditions such as drought, flood and fire have caused massive erosion in many areas.

We need to replant our continent: the branches and leaves of trees protect the soil by reducing the eroding impact of wind and rain, and the roots, fallen leaves and branches form a protective layer and enable moisture to soak slowly into the soil, so reducing the eroding effects of rapid run-off.

Timber production for profit

Australian Paper Manufacturers (APM) in conjunction with CSIRO has genetically improved seed from a number of eucalypts for commercial timber production. Three eucalypts that have been improved significantly are *Eucalyptus globulus*

(southern blue gum), *E. nitens* (shining gum) and *E. regnans* (mountain ash). Seedlings from genetically improved seed are available from APM.

Thinnings from woodlots can be used for firewood and farm posts and poles, while the quality mature trees can be sold for pulp or sawn timber at a later date.

Wildflowers as cut flowers

The variety and brilliance of our unique flora has resulted in a rapidly expanding market for native cut flowers, both in Australia and overseas.

Legislation now protects certain wildflower species from commercial picking, with national parks, State forests and wildflower reserves established to ensure that these plants survive in their wild state. However, protected species may be legally traded if they have been grown on private land.

Commercial horticulture of Australian wildflowers for the cut-flower industry is a growth area, with boronias, everlastings, waratahs, banksias, verticordias (feather flowers) and dryandras being important blooms.

Many marginal grain farms (especially in Western Australia) have changed their operation to successful wildflower production, while intensive cultivation of plants such as kangaroo paw is practised in glasshouses closer to population centres.

Smoke-bush, wax flowers, thryptomene and everlasting daisies are all long-lasting small flowers that are popular in floral displays. There is also an expanding market in dried and preserved flowers, as well as in seed pods, cones, nuts, capsules and native grass heads.

The Proteaceae family includes our most spectacular flower heads, with blooms often lasting for months. Banksias, hakeas, grevilleas and dryandras are just some of the many protea-type plants in Australia. Cross-breeding and hybridisation have produced thousands of additional spectacular strains to add to the original protea-type species.

Dramatic banksia blooms are now grown both in Australia and in Israel for the Dutch and Tokyo flower markets. In order to produce top-quality flower heads, commercial banksia farms need to be located on acidic sandy soil that is very well drained.

The potential for the native cut-flower industry is enormous, with Australian flowers and seed capable of earning major export dollars.

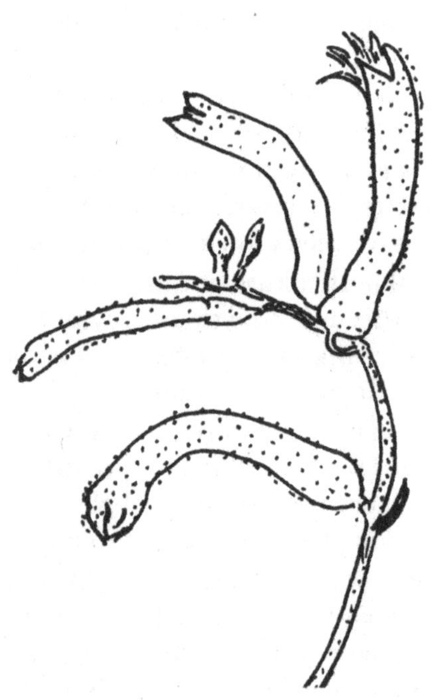

Kangaroo paw – popular native cut flower.

Shelterbelts

Shelterbelts can prevent massive stock losses in severe weather conditions, especially with newborn lambs and freshly shorn sheep. They can also reduce wind damage to fruit, grain and vegetable crops as well as increase wool, meat and milk productivity.

The usual aim is to grow trees that will filter the wind rather than act as a solid barrier, so choice of species and design of the shelterbelt are important factors. A three-row shelterbelt within a well-constructed and maintained fence is a common and successful design. Ideally it should be 20–25 times longer than the tallest tree's mature height, with a variety of species so that disease or insect attack are unlikely to destroy an entire shelterbelt.

Shrubs, medium-size trees and taller trees provide the best shelter, as the shrubs provide dense cover close to the ground, to deflect wind upwards, while the taller trees filter the wind and so reduce wind speed.

The rows should be spaced not less than 3 m apart, with 2.5 m between compact low shrubs and 8 m between the larger trees.

Any trees that die should be replaced as soon as weather conditions permit – and many species will live longer and thicken if pruned, especially the acacias.

Shelterbelts can also be successfully established by direct seeding, using locally collected seed. Natural regeneration should be encouraged as well, especially around remnant native trees where the soil will be rich in seed. These areas need to be carefully prepared, and fenced to protect the young trees. For more detail see **Direct seeding** and **Natural regeneration** in Chapter 4.

Effect of shelterbelt on wind flow.

Wildlife corridors and habitats

Seed can be used to great advantage to establish shelterbelts that will link wildlife habitats, so creating corridors through which birds, mammals, reptiles and insects will move. For example, a shelterbelt can link a dam with an area of natural roadside vegetation. Shelterbelt trees will attract the insect-eating birds that play an important role in controlling insect pests, especially pasture pests such as cockchafers.

A carefully planned shelterbelt will provide large dead trees with hollows, tall trees, low bushy trees, low shrubs and leaf litter. With this diversity there will be nesting sites, shelter and food for a wide variety of species.

Dams, lagoons and swamps provide a nucleus around which trees may be planted to create essential habitats for wildlife. Eucalypts, paperbarks, bottlebrushes, she-oaks and tea-trees suit these areas and provide valuable nectar, pollen and insect food for birds.

Trees should not be planted on a dam wall because the roots may provide channels for leakage. Near the water's edge they are best planted in clumps, to allow open areas as flight paths for birds as well as open shallow areas of water for wading birds.

Wattles provide generously for wildlife, as their abundant seeds supply food for cockatoos and parrots, wrens and native pigeons, as well as for ants. Numerous insects choose to live in foliage and many of these actually help control insects that eat the foliage and sap of neighbouring eucalypts. Some will also provide food for birds.

Acacias supply essential winter food for sugar gliders in the form of a sugary gum. *Acacia mearnsii* (black wattle) is particularly valuable in this regard, so planting the seed of this tree is very important in areas that support populations of sugar gliders.

Special projects

The eastern barred bandicoot is one of the most endangered species in Victoria, with a population of less than 150 surviving in and around the Hamilton City tip. A tree-planting project has been carried out on an unused stretch of railway line between Hamilton and Coleraine, with the aim of creating a special habitat for this rare bandicoot. A group of dedicated people have worked together with seeds and young trees to save this precious mammal species from extinction.

In a similar way, a Victorian conservation group at Nathalia is using local seed to save the rare 40 cm superb parrot from the threat of extinction. The group organised working bees to collect seed from black, grey and yellow box trees, as well as from local wattles. Members spread plastic beneath the wattles to collect the seed as the trees were shaken. Approximately 2000 seedling trees were planted in 1993 to help feed these beautiful parrots, but also for protection and future nesting sites.

Only about 100 breeding pairs of this parrot remain. The Nathalia group has a long-range program to further extend the habitat of the superb parrot, using local seed for this important work.

On French Island, in the Strathbogie Ranges, on Phillip Island and in many other places, eucalypts are being planted by people committed to the welfare of our koalas. And many of these people are collecting seed to grow their own trees.

All over Australia people are working together to save our precious fauna and flora.

We hope you will help.

*Saw banksia (*Banksia serrata*), showing open fruit.*

Appendix

An ABC of Australian plants and seeds

Acacia seed

Gathering and processing acacia seed has become an important minor industry as a result of the demand for seed to revegetate eroded areas, for large-scale plantings by direct seeding, and for quick-growing shelterbelts.

As acacias give abundant seed and grow very rapidly, it has been possible to develop a large export market for the seed. Several kilograms of seed can be harvested from quite a small tree.

With about 900 species of acacia native to Australia there is at least one species in flower in most regions throughout the entire year.

Ants make good use of acacia seed as a food source. Large concentrations of seed can be found in ants' nests buried at depths of 15 cm or more.

Acacia seed, stored in paper envelopes and bottles in the uncontrolled atmosphere of a building, have been found to be still viable after 68 years.

Age

Trees live longer and grow taller and larger in mass than any other living thing on land or sea. Eucalypts can live to a thousand years of age, Tasmanian Huon pine can live for over three thousand years.

Art and craft

After extracting the seed from nuts, cones and pods, you can make good use of the many interesting shapes and textures.

- In pottery, capsules, seeds and cones can be pressed into soft clay to give unusual imprints.
- Percussion instruments can be made using woody seed cases and large bean-like pods.
- Jewellery and buttons can be created from gumnuts, as well as from hakea and melaleuca seed pods.
- Wall hangings can be enriched by the addition of seed cases of different shapes and textures.
- Mobiles, featuring unusual seed cases and fruit, make unique decoration.
- Gift cards can be decorated with nuts, pods, cones and pressed grasses.
- Floral arrangements are enhanced by the addition of fleshy fruits, semi-dry pods, banksia cones and gumnuts.
- Interesting 'nut' creatures can be created using allocasuarina, casuarina and banksia cones, hakea nuts and gumnuts.

- Necklaces, bracelets and earrings can be made using the nut of the quandong or native peach. This beautifully textured ornamental seed has been used as bush tucker for thousands of years. Now it is being recognised for its natural beauty as well.

Birds

Birds will be attracted to trees and shrubs of the following types.

- *Acacia cyanophylla* (orange wattle) and *A. pycnantha* (golden wattle).
- *Banksia* species (honeysuckles).
- *Callistemon* species (bottlebrushes).
- *Allocasuarina* and *Casuarina* species (she-oaks, bulokes, swamp oaks).
- *Eucalyptus* species (gum trees, mallees, boxes).
- *Grevillea* species (spider flowers).
- *Hakea* species (needle-bushes).
- *Leptospermum* species (tea-trees).
- *Melaleuca* species (paperbarks or honey-myrtles).

Edible fruit and seed

Aboriginal people have traditionally used indigenous fruit as an important part of their diet; however, great care must be taken by people whose knowledge is limited, as many seeds contain toxins.

Poisonous seeds are sometimes edible if soaked or roasted, but it is unwise to experiment. Black beans, kangaroo paw and wild parsnips are particularly poisonous! The following are some Australian fruit and seed that are edible.

- Acacia seeds can be ground between stones for baking, or the immature wattle pods may be lightly roasted. (The gelatinous acacia gum can also be eaten.)
- The black plum (*Diospyros australis*) has black ovoid fruit 1.5 cm long.
- The quandong or native peach (*Santalum acuminatum*) produces bright red fruit that can be eaten raw or used to make jam or jelly. The kernel can also be eaten. The plum-bush or northern sandalwood (*Santalum lanceolatum*) produces succulent purple-blue fruit that is a recognised Aboriginal food. All *Santalum* species produce edible fruit.
- The blue quandong (*Elaeocarpus grandis*) bears bright-blue fruit and grows in rainforests in New South Wales and Queensland.
- The boobiallas (*Myoporum* species) produce small juicy berries – without much flavour.
- Coastal noonflower (*Carpobrotus glaucescens*) is a succulent groundcover with deep-red fruit that has a refreshing taste.
- The native tamarinds (*Diploglottis campbellii* and *Diploglottis australis*) have juicy red or yellow fruit for eating raw or for putting in drink or jam.

- Elderberries (*Sambucus* species) may be used to make wine, or may be eaten raw.
- Muntries (*Kunzea pomifera*) yield small, succulent purplish fruit that is an Aboriginal food and was used by white settlers for fruit tarts.
- Lilly-pilly (*Acmena/Eugenia* species) produce crisp pink fruit that is rather tasteless but excellent for jelly.
- The nut of *Macadamia integrifolia* is Australia's most widely accepted edible fruit.
- *Melastroma affine* and other *Melastroma* species have edible sweet black berries.
- The midgen berry (*Austromyrtus dulcis*) has white or mauve fruit that is sweet and edible. *Austromyrtus tenuifolia* has edible bluish fruit. Both are good for jam.
- The cherry ballart (*Exocarpus cupressiformis*) produces small green hard fruit that is sweet and tasty when ripened to a deep red.
- The leafless currant bush (*Leptorneria aphylla*) produces small green succulent fruit. Eat raw in the spring.
- Quena (*Solanum esuriale*) yields yellow berries 10–15 mm in diameter. These may be roasted or eaten raw.
- The cranberry heath (*Astroloma humifusum*) yields small greenish fruit.
- The native finger lime (*Microcitrus australasica*) bears long, cylindrical fruit that has an orange-like flavour. Eat raw or make into marmalade.
- Native raspberries (*Rubus* species) supply raspberry-like fruit.
- The pepper bush (*Tasmannia insipida*) has small purple fruit. The flesh is edible but bland, while the seeds are hot in flavour.
- The riberry (*Syzygium luehmannii*) has pear-shaped, pink to red fruit 1–2 cm long. It is good for jams or sauces.

- Old man saltbush (*Atriplex nummularia*) gives massive quantities of seed after flowering. This seed may be ground into flour, mixed with water then cooked as damper in the coals of a fire.

Floral emblems

Australia's floral emblem is the acacia, usually *Acacia pycnantha* (golden wattle). States also have floral emblems, as follows.

- New South Wales: *Telopea speciosissima* (NSW waratah).
- Northern Territory: *Gossypium sturtianum* (Sturts desert rose). An hibiscus-like mauve flower with a red centre.
- Queensland: *Dendrobium bigibbum* (Cooktown orchid).
- South Australia: *Clianthus formosus* (Sturt desert pea).
- Tasmania: *Eucalyptus globulus* (Tasmanian blue gum).
- Victoria: *Epacris impressa* (pink common heath).
- Western Australia: *Anigozanthos manglesii* (Red-stemmed green kangaroo paw).

Flowers for every month of the calendar year

- January: *Eucalyptus ficifolia* (red flowering gum).
- February: *Callistemon brachyandrus* (prickly bottlebrush).
- March: *Hakea laurina* (pincushion hakea).
- April: *Banksia spinulosa* (hill or hairpin banksia).
- May: *Banksia ericifolia* (heath banksia).
- June: *Eucalyptus caesia* (gungurru).

- July: *Acacia podalyriaefolia* (Queensland silver wattle).
- August: *Acacia baileyana* (Cootamundra wattle).
- September: *Calothamnus villosus* (woolly net-bush).
- October: *Melaleuca fulgens* (scarlet honey-myrtle).
- November: *Callistemon speciosus* (common bottlebrush).
- December: *Melaleuca hypericifolia* (red honey-myrtle).

Mangrove seed

There are about thirty species of mangrove in Australia. They have fruit that float, to enable the seed to scatter by water. Some seed germinates while still attached to the parent plant.

Partly developed seedlings are often seen washed up on beaches with their developing root structure and bright green leaves attached to the seed, which resembles a lima bean.

Seed potential

- Two kilograms of mixed native seed has the potential to become over 6000 plants, enough vegetation to plant 2 ha of new bushland habitat, or 7 km of direct-seeded wildlife corridor.

Seed weight

- One kilogram of acacia seed contains about 50,000 seeds; one kilogram of eucalypt seed contains about 500,000; and one kilogram of melaleuca or callistemon seed contains about 1,000,000 seeds.

- Five wheelbarrows of eucalypt twigs (containing nuts but without much leaf) will give about one kilogram of seed. Two wheelbarrows of allocasuarina or casuarina cones will give over one kilogram of seed.
- To get half a kilogram of acacia seed requires steady picking of pods for a good half hour.
- One marri (*Eucalyptus calophylla*) seed weighs one-seventh of a gram.

Unique seed capsules

As 80 per cent of Australian plants are native to Australia alone, most of our seed capsules are unique.

Water consumption

- A mature eucalypt uses 100–120 litres of water daily.
- One tree can use up 3200 litres of water in a month; 6000 mature trees will prevent 241 million litres of water a year from entering the watertable beneath a farming property.

Index

Acknowledgements

Michael Lloyd of Kings Park and Botanic Garden, Perth, Western Australia, generously provided us with information regarding smoke stimulated seed germination. In addition, Michael checked the smoke section of Chapter 3, for accuracy.

Keith Johnson and Phil Graham of Tecnica Pty Ltd (who produce Regen 2000 Smokemaster, Direct and Seed Starter) provided us with additional information regarding smoke stimulated seed germination, and their product. Also, Keith Johnson checked this section of Chapter 3, for accuracy. Tecnica Pty Ltd are located at 9 Newcastle Road, Bayswater, Victoria 3153.

About the authors

Douglas Stewart grew up in Melbourne, trained as an engineer and taught science and agricultural science in secondary schools in country Victoria. He has spent the last fifteen years as a farmer. A practical man at heart, Doug has always had an interest in collecting and germinating Australian plants for use on degraded land. His interest in conservation and the propagation of trees is long-standing, and he is involved in the Landcare movement.

Robin Stewart was born in Melbourne and has travelled extensively in Australia and overseas. She has a passion for plants and animals, which she has combined with a career as a writer and teacher.

Robin and Doug spent seven years farming sheep on King Island, where they established a penguin-banding program and bred and showed Irish Setters. Back on the mainland they bred stud Angus cattle in Central Victoria, before moving to Phillip Island in 1996. They now live a double life: six months on Phillip Island and six months in Mitchell, in outback Queensland. On the island, Robin writes full-time, while at the same time studying muttonbirds and penguins and helping to revegetate a nearby muttonbird rookery. In Mitchell, Robin and Doug are involved in collecting seed to grow into native trees and shrubs that will survive and thrive in this arid region.